United Nations

Department of Economic and Social Affairs
Statistics

Natural Capital Accounting For Integrated Biodiversity Policies

© United Nations, 2020

© United Nations, 2020

All rights reserved worldwide

Requests to reproduce excerpts or to photocopy should be addressed to the Copyright Clearance Center at copyright.com.

All other queries on rights and licenses, including subsidiary rights, should be addressed to: United Nations Publications, 405 East 42nd St, S-09FW001, New York, NY 10017, United States of America. Email: permissions@un.org; website: shop.un.org

The findings, interpretations, and conclusions expressed herein are those of the author(s) and do not necessarily reflect the views of the United Nations or its officials or Member States.

URL Links contained in the present publication are provided for the convenience of the reader and are correct at the time of issue. The United Nations takes no responsibility for the continued accuracy of that information or for the content of any external website.

United Nations publication issued by Department of Economic and Social Affairs.

With funding from the Federal Ministry for Economic Cooperation and Development of Germany, www.bmz.de, implemented by Deutsche Gesellschaft fur Internationale Zusammenarbeit (GIZ) GmbH, www.giz.de.

With funding from the
Federal Ministry for Economic Cooperation and Development

Supported by

giz Deutsche Gesellschaft für Internationale Zusammenarbeit (GIZ) GmbH

ISBN: 978-92-1-259156-8

eISBN: 978-92-1-005252-8

Sales No: E.20.XVII.16

United Nations | Department of Economic and Social Affairs

The Department of Economic and Social Affairs of the United Nations Secretariat is a vital interface between global policies in the economic, social and environmental spheres and national action. The Department works in three main interlinked areas: it compiles, generates and analyses a wide range of economic, social and environmental data and information on which Member States of the United Nations draw to review common problems and to take stock of policy options; it facilitates the negotiations of Member States in many intergovernmental bodies on joint courses of action to address ongoing or emerging global challenges; and it advises interested Governments on the ways and means of translating policy frameworks developed in United Nations conferences and summits into programmes at the country level and, through technical assistance, helps build national capacities.

The Statistics Division of the Department of Economic and Social Affairs is a global centre for data on all subject matters, bringing to the world statistical information compiled by the entire UN system. It is committed to the advancement of the global statistical system, by compiling and disseminating global statistical information, developing standards and norms for statistical activities, and supporting countries' efforts to strengthen their national statistical systems. It also facilitates the coordination of international statistical activities and supports the functioning of the United Nations Statistical Commission.

The System of Environmental-Economic Accounting (SEEA) is the first international statistical standard for environmental-economic accounting, which was adopted by the United Nations Statistical Commission at its 43rd Session in 2012. The SEEA brings together economic and environmental information into a common framework to measure the contribution of the environment to the economy, the impact of the economy on the environment, and the condition of the ecosystems and the services they provide.

For further information on the SEEA, please visit seea.un.org or contact seea@un.org.

CONTENTS

EXECUTIVE SUMMARY

Photo: John Bode00 Castillo

Biodiversity plays an essential role and represents a key component towards sustaining human societies, our well well-being and our global economy. Its importance has often been overlooked and taken for granted, not just by decision-makers, but also by humans as a collective. As a result, we are now experiencing some of the biggest declines in biodiversity of our time.

In order to safeguard its future, it is essential that there is an increased global effort to better understand, not only the drivers behind this rapid loss, but also the interlinkages and interactions that exist across the three pillars of sustainability - society, economy and environment. With this knowledge at hand, and by asking the right policy questions, decision-makers can make more informed policy decisions around tackling these drivers, as well as the impacts of this ongoing biodiversity loss. The most relevant biodiversity policy questions are those linked to land use change; exploitation/overexploitation of animals, plants and other organisms, mainly via harvesting, logging, hunting and fishing; climate change; and pollution.

Biodiversity is the engine that drives the flow of benefits from natural capital to humanity. Thus, when it comes to decision-making around biodiversity issues, there is a broad range of different groups – public and private – that would benefit from being able to take on board ecosystems and ecosystem services more comprehensively. A whole systems approach allows these decision-makers to identify the linkages between policy domains but also account for the overall outcomes of decisions. Natural capital accounting (NCA) is an approach which integrates the environment into a more holistic policy analysis through the compilation of environmental-economic accounts.

The international statistical standard for NCA is the System of Environmental-Economic Accounting (SEEA), which organizes and presents statistics on the environment and its relationship with the economy. The SEEA framework follows a similar accounting structure as the System of National Accounts (SNA), the international statistical standard for macroeconomic statistics. One of the main benefits of the SEEA is that it uses a systems approach to provide a wide range of data, including data on ecosystems and species as well as on drivers of biodiversity loss and policy responses. It can also provide information on the drivers and impacts of biodiversity simultaneously. Users, therefore, can rely on a single system to understand drivers, impacts, responses, and importantly, the effectiveness of policy responses. In addition, whilst ecosystems-level biodiversity is already at the core of the SEEA, the UN Committee of Experts on Environmental-Economic Accounting (UNCEEA) is currently undertaking work to ensure that biodiversity at all levels, including species and genes, is better reflected moving forward.

Background

AUDIENCE

This paper is aimed at policymakers at various levels, including international organizations, national governments and local authorities, who are responsible for creating and implementing biodiversity policies or policies that are dependent upon or impact biodiversity. This document will demonstrate the importance of natural capital accounting (NCA) by way of the System of Environmental-Economic Accounting (SEEA) in the formulation of effective biodiversity policy, with a focus on those policies that relate to ecosystems, ecosystem services and species.

Biodiversity is critical for both human well-being as well as for the economy. Based on this notion, it is a misconception to think that effective biodiversity policies can be pursued in a silo, without any meaningful understanding of the inter-relationship between the environment, the economy and society. Similarly, it is also a misconception to think that concerns over biodiversity should be addressed solely through policies that promote protected areas or dedicated conservation efforts. A wide range of policies - from international to local - across a variety of sectors, stand to benefit from using the SEEA framework because it uncovers the interrelationships between different policy domains and ongoing environmental developments. Thus, this paper is not aimed exclusively at biodiversity policymakers; it also discusses how economic and social policies can be improved and integrated, and therefore also appeals to other government ministries such as finance ministries.

In addition to policymakers, this paper may be of interest to businesses, NGOs, banks, insurance companies or members of the general public. For example, the corporate sector is increasingly adopting NCA in their decision-making processes in order to understand their dependencies on biodiversity and de-risk supply chains.[1] While the focus of examples in this paper are mainly on country-level applications that appeal to national governments, some examples are also relevant to other stakeholder groups.

Also related to this issue paper is an overview paper on the applications of the SEEA to policy and two separate papers on climate change and macro-economic policies, which are targeted towards more specific audiences. The paper on macro-economic policy is meant for finance ministries or central banks that want to understand both the

---

[1] Although companies are adopting NCA it is not always done using SEEA methodology (see also Example 4). There are however efforts to find common ground so that the various approaches align (Spurgeon et al., 2018).

short and long-term impacts of the environment on economic growth. The issue papers on climate change is geared towards environmental policymakers who are interested in the value that the SEEA can bring to their domain.

THE ENHANCA PROJECT

This paper is part of a series that has been developed by the project "EnhaNCA: Enhance Natural Capital Accounting Policy Uptake and Relevance" which provides materials to increase policymakers' understanding of policy applications of NCA according to the SEEA. The objective of the project is to address three shortcomings in the environmental and economic policy space:

(a) A lack of awareness by policy makers on the value added of NCA and how it can address policy needs;
(b) A lack of systemization of the potential applications of NCA; and
(c) A lack of compelling case studies on the impact of NCA policy applications.

ACKNOWLEDGEMENTS

The project has received generous support from the German Federal Ministry for Economic Cooperation and Development, implemented through the Deutsche Gesellschaft für Internationale Zusammenarbeit (GIZ) GmbH.

This paper has been authored by David Coates, Jessica Ying Chan (United Nations Statistics Division) and Chloe Hill (Altus Impact) under the guidance of an editorial board. The Editorial Board operated under the direction of Alessandra Alfieri (United Nations Statistics Division) and included the following persons: Thomas Brookes (IUCN), Raffaello Cervigni (World Bank), Glenn-Marie Lange (World Bank), Wadzanayi Mandivenyi (Department of Environmental Affairs of South Africa), Stefano Pagiola (World Bank), Corli Pretorius (UNEP-WCMC) and Juha Siikamaki (IUCN), and was chaired by A.H. Kroese (Statistics Netherlands).

The authors and editorial board would like to acknowledge the inputs of Sarah K. Jones (Altus Impact) for her design services on this paper. The author and editorial board would also like to acknowledge the support and contributions of Nina Bisom and Johannes Kruse (GIZ) in producing this paper.

With funding from the

Supported by

Acronyms

CBD	Convention on Biological Diversity
CO$_2$	Carbon dioxide
GDP	Gross Domestic Product
IPBES	Intergovernmental Science-Policy Platform on Biodiversity and Ecosystem Services
NCA	Natural capital account(ing)
PAs	Protected areas
PES	Payment for ecosystem services
REDD+	UN Collective Programme on Reducing Emissions from Deforestation and Forest Degradation in Developing Countries
SEEA	System of Environmental-Economic Accounting
SEEA CF	System of Environmental-Economic Accounting - Central Framework
SEEA EEA	System of Environmental-Economic Accounting - Experimental Ecosystem Accounting
SNA	System of National Accounts
SDGs	Sustainable Development Goals
UN	United Nations
UNCEEA	United Nations Committee of Experts on Environmental - Economic Accounting

photo : Geio Tischler

1. INTRODUCTION

Biodiversity plays a fundamental role towards sustaining life on Earth. Representing a key element of any country's natural capital[2] stock, biodiversity contributes to the maintenance and delivery of critical ecosystem services upon which our economies and societies depend. Even though this has been common knowledge for quite some time, biodiversity's value has often not been fully captured or recognized in policy decisions (TEEB, 2011).

This biodiversity "undervaluation" has meant that we still bear witness to its continual destruction and loss, where a range of indirect and direct drivers (causes), which are mainly underpinned by unsustainable economic activities, remain the key culprits. If we are to protect our planet and ensure our own future well-being, we need to better understand the interlinkages between this environment-economy nexus (OECD, 2019a) and start asking the right policy questions that can lead to informed policy decisions that tackle both the drivers and impacts of biodiversity loss.

Without establishing the connection between ecosystems and the economy, we 1) cannot have a good understanding of what is ultimately driving biodiversity loss and 2) cannot understand what policies are needed to ensure the well-being of society and how to better manage biodiversity to achieve more sustainable and efficient economies. In order to address these biodiversity challenges, collective fundamental societal transformations are required that are based on innovative thinking and integrated polices. To do this, we need to manage capital (natural, social, human and produced) in a way that enhances human well-being over the short and long term.

Biodiversity is a challenging and complex policy area. The Agenda 2030 for Sustainable Development[3], an integrated agenda for sustainability, provides a necessary starting point for decision-makers, by acknowledging the interactions across the three pillars of sustainability -society, economy and environment. As it is impossible to make effective policies by looking at these pillars in silos, a whole systems approach is required. A systems approach allows policymakers to identify the linkages between policy domains, but also accounts for the overall outcomes of decisions. Natural capital accounting (NCA) is an approach which

---

[2] Natural capital is the stock of renewable and non-renewable resources (e.g. plants, animals, air, water, soils, fossil fuels, minerals) that combine to yield a flow of benefits to people. The concept of natural capital extends beyond nature as a source of raw materials for production (e.g. timber) to include the role of the environment in supporting human well-being through the supply of such important goods and services as clean water, fertile soils and valuable genetic resources (United Nations, 2014a).

[3] The 2030 Agenda for Sustainable Development was agreed upon in 2015. See: https://sustainabledevelopment.un.org/

does exactly that: by integrating the environment into a more holistic policy analysis through the compilation of environmental-economic accounts. The agreed framework for NCA is the System of Environmental-Economic Accounts (SEEA), which is the accepted international statistical standard for organizing and presenting statistics on the environment and its relationship with the economy. The SEEA framework follows a similar accounting structure as the System of National Accounts (SNA), the international statistical standard for macroeconomic statistics.

For effective biodiversity policymaking, it is important to look at the drivers and impacts simultaneously. The SEEA can provide information on both. For example, for impacts, the SEEA can measure changes in ecosystem extent, condition and services. What ecosystems are being degraded, where, how other ecosystems are improving or declining in condition and the impact on the supply of ecosystem services. For drivers, the accounts can show what economic activities are driving ecosystem degradation. The SEEA suite of accounts can show, for example, how farmers benefit from ecosystem services for crops production (ecosystem service accounts) but also how condition is degrading in these same areas (ecosystem condition accounts), perhaps up to the point where the actual monetary value of the ecosystem begins to decline (ecosystem asset accounts).

This paper looks at the policy questions, as well as the information and data that are required for more effective biodiversity policies. It does this by focusing on how NCA, using the SEEA, can play a vital role in improving the state of biodiversity and ensuring the delivery of essential ecosystem services. This paper

is not, however, an extensive view of this topic. For instance, it does not attempt to review the "intrinsic value" or "existence value" of biodiversity, nor other non-tangible values of biodiversity such as "religious and cultural values". Rather, its purpose is to raise awareness of the opportunities for the SEEA to assist with making effective and sustainable policy decisions.

To do this, the paper first explains what biodiversity is, how it is considered in an economic context, and summarizes the current biodiversity trends and drivers of loss and how this affects sustainable development more broadly (part 1). It then looks at the key biodiversity policy questions that need to be asked, followed by an overview of the institutional landscape and stakeholder challenges in this realm (part 2). The paper then looks at the biodiversity policy responses and instruments in more detail, including the role of the SEEA (part 3). The final part of the paper illustrates, using real world examples, how the SEEA can respond to policy information for biodiversity and how to move forward to enable effective policymaking, including a discussion of further innovations required (part 4). It is hoped that the paper may result in increased demand for NCA inputs into policy dialogue and hence increased support for compilation of the SEEA.

photo : Andrew Coelho

2. THE POLICY CONTEXT

2.1 What is Biodiversity and Why Does it Matter?

The term "biodiversity" is the contracted form of "biological diversity" which is defined as the variability among living organisms from all sources including, inter alia, terrestrial, marine and other aquatic ecosystems and the ecological complexes of which they are part; this includes diversity within species, between species and of ecosystems (Article 2, Convention on Biological Diversity 1992).

There is a close relationship between ecological and species diversity: species depend on ecosystems, but species also influence the condition and characteristics of ecosystems. For example, large herbivores influence the ecological character and condition of natural grasslands. Diversity "within species" refers to genetic diversity such as various strains, varieties or breeds of the same species of animal or plant. Genetic diversity is extremely important and vital to sustaining biodiversity itself. Not only is it the basis of natural selection and evolution, it is a very important aspect of the current benefits associated with biodiversity and particularly in agriculture, food and nutrition (FAO, 2019).

In an economic context, biodiversity is the engine that drives the flow of benefits from natural capital to humanity. This "flow" is driven by ecosystem services that deliver benefits such as crop provisioning, water regulation and cultural services. No matter if biodiversity is considered to be at the level of ecosystems, species or genes - the link to economics is, at the end, through ecosystem services. However, it is important to note that biodiversity, in this paper, largely refers to ecosystem-level diversity (and at times species-level diversity).

Ecosystems can be natural, semi-natural, artificial or managed. Some countries have no natural areas remaining but nevertheless their modified landscapes still provide valuable ecosystem services. For example, ecosystem services provided by blue/green areas within urban ecosystems provide valuable recreation and air purification services. Some ecosystem services, such as those derived from agricultural ecosystems, depend on human management for their existence. NCA does not, therefore, pre-judge what kind or status of biodiversity or ecosystem is best, but includes all ecosystem services no matter how or where they are delivered.

One estimate puts the notional global economic value of ecosystem services at USD 125 trillion per year, around two-thirds higher than global gross domestic product (GDP) (Costanza et al., 2014). Other than provisioning services, most ecosystem services are non-marketed and therefore not included in most economic accounting. Clearly, then, biodiversity is a central component for a healthy economy and therefore needs to be properly included in accounting.

As biodiversity underpins the functioning of ecosystem services, its loss translates into social and economic consequences. The costs of inaction on biodiversity loss are high. Between 1997 and 2011, the world lost an estimated USD 4-20 trillion per year in ecosystem services owing to land-cover change alone and an estimated USD 6-11 trillion per year from land degradation (OECD, 2015). By combining likelihood and impact, the World Economic Forum (WEF) (2019) ranked biodiversity loss and ecosystem collapse in the top five of the highest global economic risks. The accelerating pace of biodiversity loss, therefore, has been identified as a particular concern to the global economy and collective human well-being (World Economic Forum, 2019).

2.2 Biodiversity Trends and Drivers of its Loss

The recent Global Assessment Report on Biodiversity and Ecosystem Services by the Intergovernmental Science Policy Platform on Biodiversity and Ecosystem Services (IPBES) paints a bleak picture of the global state of biodiversity (see Figure 1 below).

Figure 1: *Extinctions since 1500*

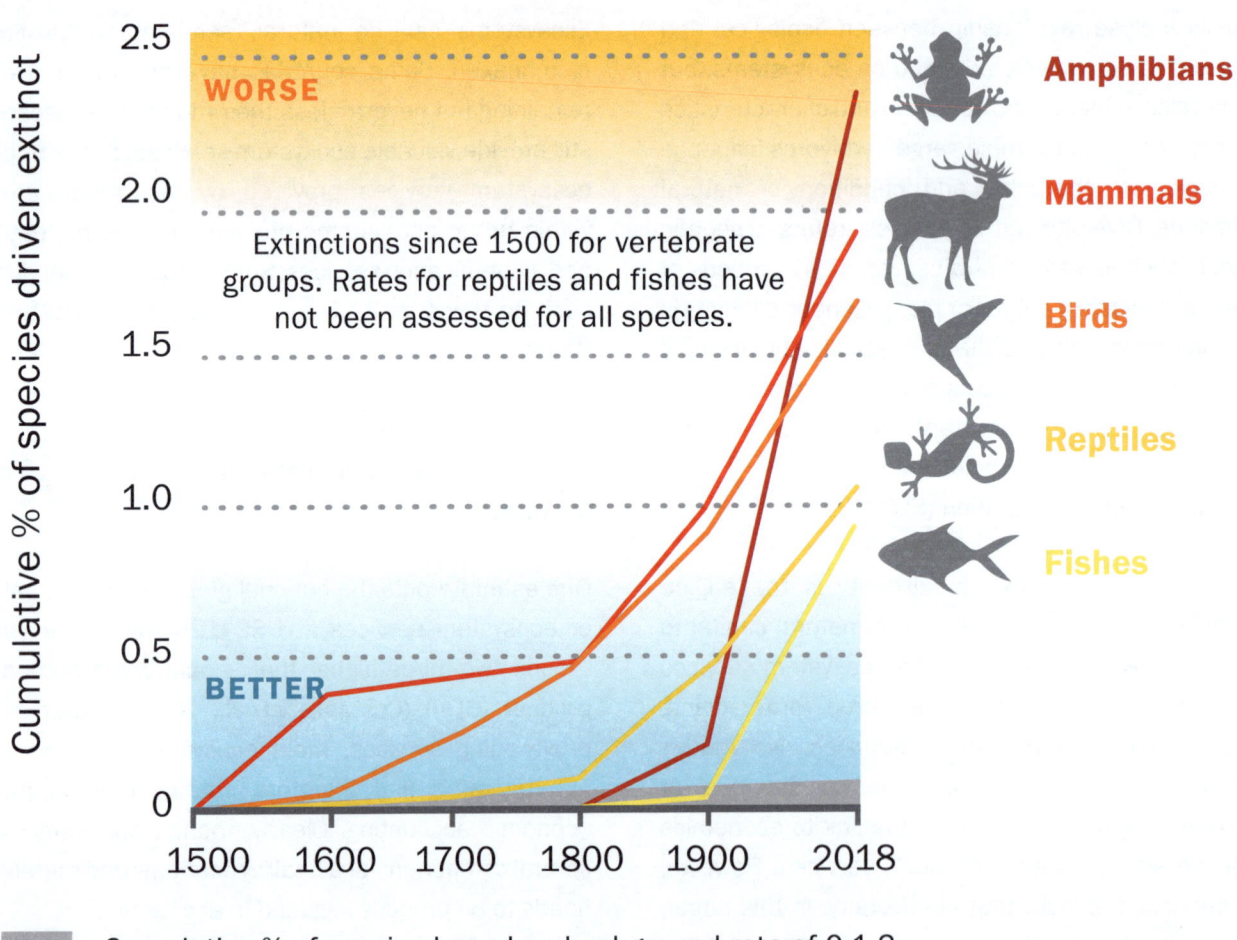

Cumulative % of species based on background rate of 0.1-2 extinctions per million species per year

Source: IPBES, 2019

A vast majority of the report's findings show a continued rapid decline of biodiversity: for example, 75 per cent of the land surface is significantly altered, 66 per cent of the ocean area is experiencing increasing cumulative impacts, over 85 per cent of wetland area has been lost. Furthermore, the IUCN Red List[®] of Threatened Species reveals that about a quarter of species in comprehensively assessed groups face a high risk of extinction in the near future (IPBES, 2019). Genetic diversity, and notably that required to support sustainable farming, continues to decline (FAO, 2019). Out of the 16 categories of "nature's contributions to people"[4] that have been assessed, and that were identified in the recent IPBES report, 13 categories continue to be in decline (IPBES, 2019). Only 3 of these categories - 1) energy, 2) food and feed and 3) materials and assistance - show an overall increase, but even these trends vary among regions, with some regions experiencing declines in contributions.

Progress towards internationally agreed biodiversity targets (see Section 3.1), or sub-targets, has been positive in only five instances out of 53[5]. Current negative trends in biodiversity will also undermine progress towards 80 per cent of the assessed targets of the Sustainable Development Goals (SDGs) related to poverty, hunger, health, water, cities, climate, oceans and land (IPBES, 2019). Similarly, given the close relationship between biodiversity and climate,

declines in biodiversity will undoubtedly undermine the goals specified in the Paris Agreement on Climate Change.

Importantly, progress towards addressing the underlying causes of biodiversity loss and reducing direct pressures on biodiversity has been overwhelmingly poor. The five direct drivers or causes of biodiversity loss with the largest global impact have been (starting with those with most impact): changes in land and sea use; direct exploitation of organisms; climate change; pollution; and invasion of alien species (IPBES, 2019). Food systems[6] stand out as the leading driver of biodiversity loss: for example, they account for an estimated 70 per cent of the projected loss of terrestrial biodiversity by 2050, and 50 per cent of freshwater biodiversity loss, based on current trajectories (Leadley et al., 2014). In addition, climate change is increasingly exacerbating the impact of other drivers on nature and human well-being. These five direct drivers result from an array of underlying causes – the indirect drivers of change – which are in turn underpinned by societal values and behaviours that include production and consumption patterns, human population dynamics and trends, trade, technological innovations and local through global governance. A major factor behind all these drivers is the failure to adequately include accounting for biodiversity in economic planning and investment.

---

[4] "Nature's contributions to people" is defined as "all the positive contributions, or benefits, and occasionally negative contributions, losses or detriments, that people obtain from nature" (Pascual et al., 2017). Ecosystem services are one of many of "nature's contributions to people" and the main focus of this paper.

[5] Two relating to progress towards establishing protected areas and for three process related targets (invasive alien species prioritized, protocols adopted and plans in place).

[6] Meaning both the way food is produced, including land use change and practices, and food consumption patterns.

photo : Ricardo Gomez Angel

2.3 Biodiversity Policy Questions

According to the 2019 IPBES report, "the implementation of policy responses and actions to conserve nature and manage it more sustainably has progressed, yielding positive outcomes relative to scenarios of no intervention, but progress is not sufficient to stem the direct and indirect drivers of nature deterioration".[7]

This means that not only must the direct drivers be tackled, but decision-makers must also have a solid grasp of the indirect drivers and how exactly they relate and interconnect with environmental impacts. Without this understanding, effective policy responses cannot be drawn up to address these issues. This section outlines some key policy questions/areas for the most relevant drivers that can be informed by the SEEA – land use change, (over)exploitation of organisms, climate change and pollution.

2.3.1 Linking drivers and impacts of land use change

Agricultural expansion is the most widespread form of land use change, with over one third of the terrestrial land surface being used for cropping or animal husbandry (IPBES, 2019). However, there are significant trade-offs that come with this change in land use, which are often not taken into account. If natural forest is to be turned into agricultural cropland, it is possible

that crop provisioning services are gained and GDP is increased. However, this gain may come at a cost to other ecosystem services. For example, regulating services (e.g. flood protection/mitigation, soil retention services) or cultural services (e.g. providing forests to hike in) may well disappear as a result of this change in land use. Even though these services do not appear directly in GDP, they provide considerable benefits to humanity and human well-being.

Also, according to IPBES, this expansion, coupled with a doubling of urban areas (including an expansion of infrastructure to meet the demands of a growing population), has come mostly at the expense of forests (largely old-growth tropical forests), wetlands and grasslands. Whilst urban areas still provide ecosystem services through green and blue spaces [8], it is important for decision-makers to understand how this measures up with the ecosystem services that the original land can provide, as well as any changes in the beneficiaries *(see Box 1)*.

---

[7] In the context of the IPBES report and this paper, direct drivers refer to drivers, both natural and anthropogenic, which affect nature directly, such as extreme weather events. Indirect drivers usually do not affect nature directly, but rather through their effects on direct anthropogenic drivers, for example, institutions and governance arrangements.

[8] Green spaces can be defined as all urban land covered by vegetation of any kind, whether on private or public grounds, and irrespective of size and function. Blue spaces include small water bodies in urban areas, such as ponds, lakes or streams (World Health Organization Regional Office for Europe, 2017).

Photo : Deny Ekayana

Box 1: The Value of Urban Tree Canopies in Oslo

To give an example of ecosystem services in urban areas, tree canopy is the most important green structure by surface area in the built up area of Oslo. There is an increasing awareness about the value of urban tree canopies and their contribution to urban life quality, neighbourhood cohesion, wildlife habitat and ecosystem services such as air pollution mitigation, carbon storage, run off control and temperature regulation. However, in order to ensure the flow of ecosystem services from these trees, it is necessary to know where they are and what condition they are in. There is therefore an increasing demand for cost-effective and standardised procedures for automated production of high-resolution tree canopy maps (Hanssen, 2019).

2.3.2 (Over)exploitation of animals, plants and other organisms, mainly via harvesting, logging, hunting and fishing

Since the 1970s, not only has the global human population on Earth doubled, but the global economy has also grown nearly fourfold. Moreover, global trade has grown tenfold and led to greater disconnect between where production occurs versus where goods are consumed. Together, this has increased the collective demand for energy and materials and increased natural resource exploitation rates in new ways that need to be taken into consideration when designing policy.

In relation to the policy questions surrounding (over) exploitation, the impact on biodiversity needs to be taken into account to ensure sustainable development. For example: what consequences do harvesting/logging/hunting/fishing have for overall ecosystem health? At what point do these activities become unsustainable and can no longer guarantee future provision of these ecosystem services? When considering such questions, it is also important to note that the value of ecosystem services, in this case, is not just about the provision of food and/or raw materials. Indeed, some species are valued on their aesthetics and contribution to human well-being. Such species may support important nature tourism opportunities

and associated revenue streams, counterbalancing the issue of over exploitation (King et al., 2016). The concerning trends of (over)exploitation beg the question: at what point are we destroying "ecosystem resilience" [9] and the ecosystem itself? When will we reach the "tipping point" of no return? By starting to ask such questions, policymakers can start to formulate more tailored policies, both nationally and sub-nationally, that tackle such issues.

2.3.3 Climate change and biodiversity

Climate change is now a well-known and well-evidenced phenomenon. According to a 2018 IPCC report, "human activities are estimated to have caused approximately 1.0°C above pre-industrial levels". Moreover, there is high confidence that global warming will reach 1.5°C, between 2030 and 2052, if it continues to increase at the current rate. As a result, this warming, caused primarily from emissions from human activity, will have a persistent effect over time and across the globe. These effects will likely persist for centuries to millennia and cause further long-term changes in the climate system, such as sea level rise (IPCC, 2018).

Biodiversity is incredibly vulnerable to climate change. Even a decade ago, the CDB (2010) noted that "climate change is already forcing biodiversity to adapt either through shifting habitat, changing life cycles, or the

---

[9] The ability of ecosystems to tolerate shocks and disturbance while maintaining the same level of functioning is often referred to as "ecosystem resilience" (Mori et al., 2013).

development of new physical traits". Today, these patterns continue to impact biodiversity, particularly for species distribution, phenology, population dynamics, community structure and ecosystem function. The compounding effects of the different drivers of change combined further exacerbate the negative impacts on nature which can already be seen across major biomes, from artic systems to coral reefs (IPBES, 2019). Biodiversity maintenance and preservation, however, is key to reducing the negative effects of climate change and adapting to it. For example, the conservation and restoration of ecosystems not only helps to remove carbon dioxide from the atmosphere, but it can also help society reduce flooding and the impacts of storm surges (CBD, 2010).

Forest ecosystems, for instance, are a stabilising force for the climate. Not only do forests serve as habitats for a diverse range of species, but they also play an integral part in the carbon cycle, support livelihoods and supply goods and services that can drive sustainable growth (IUCN, 2017). However, they are both a source and a solution for greenhouse gas emissions, making their role in climate change two-fold. The second largest source of greenhouse gas emissions comes from land use change, which accounts for around 25 per cent of global emissions. Approximately half of this 25 per cent comes from deforestation and forest degradation. Standing forests on the other hand are one of the most important solutions to addressing the effects of climate change. Reducing deforestation and forest degradation lowers GHG emissions, with an estimated mitigation potential of 0.4–5.8 gigatons of CO_2 per year (IPCC, 2019). Increasing and maintaining forests is therefore an essential solution to climate change. With nearly two billion hectares of degraded land across the world, which is approximately the size of South America, there are also plenty of opportunities for land restoration. Halting the loss and degradation of forest ecosystems and promoting their restoration have the potential to contribute to over one third of the total climate change

mitigation that scientists say is required by 2030 to meet the objectives of the Paris Agreement (IUCN, 2017). The policy question that needs to be asked here, therefore, is: how can ecosystem conservation and restoration be boosted and leveraged to combat climate change mitigation and adaptation?

2.3.4 Pollution

Pollutants which range from greenhouse gas emissions, nutrient run-off from agriculture, untreated urban, rural and industrial wastewater to oil spills and toxic dumping have had strong negative effects on soil, freshwater and marine ecosystems as well as the global atmosphere (IPBES, 2019). For example, a direct consequence of heavy air pollution is the increase of premature deaths. A large number of deaths occur in densely populated regions with high concentrations of PM2.5[10] and ozone, especially China and India, and in regions with aging populations, such as China and Eastern Europe. The OECD projected an increase in the number of premature deaths, as a result of outdoor air pollution, from approximately 3 million people in 2010, in line with the latest Global Burden of Disease estimates, to 6-9 million annually in 2060 (OECD, 2016).

Pollutants can have a large economic cost for countries. For example, a staggering USD 1.6 trillion is the economic cost of the approximate 600,000 premature deaths and diseases caused by air pollution in the WHO European Region in 2010, according to the first-ever study of these costs conducted for the Region. The amount is nearly equivalent to one tenth of the GDP of the entire European Union in 2013 (WHO & OECD, 2015).

Marine plastic pollution has also become a major issue over the last few decades, and has increased tenfold since 1980. This has affected at least 267 species, including 86 per cent of marine turtles, 44 per cent of

---

10 PM2.5 (particulate matter 2.5) are tiny particles in the air that reduce visibility and cause the air to appear hazy when levels are elevated. These particles cause air pollution and are typically a concern for people's health when levels are high.

seabirds and 43 per cent of marine mammals (IPBES, 2019). Humans have also been affected, not only through impacts on food chains but also with impacts on recreation and tourism e.g. the closing of beaches such as Maya Bay in Thailand made famous by the film "the Beach". According to an article in The Guardian (2018), due to pollution from litter as well as sun cream in the water created by the 5000 daily visitors, "it is estimated that more than 80 per cent of the coral around Maya Bay has been destroyed... despite evidence of the mounting damage to Maya Bay, for years, Thai authorities had been reluctant to shut it, because the location generates about 400 million baht (£9.5m) in revenue a year". The policy question that needs to be asked here, therefore, is: At what point do the costs arising from the economic activities behind these impacts start to outweigh the benefits? And how can we harness biodiversity and ecosystem services to mitigate and regulate pollution?

2.4 The Institutional Landscape

Historically, attitudes towards key policy questions regarding biodiversity have echoed the evolution of the "environment versus development" debate, which was often articulated in the form of a trade-off paradigm where biodiversity loss (or environment) was an unfortunate but necessary cost of economic and social advancement. Today, this debate has evolved and biodiversity considerations are no longer the sole purview of "environment" ministries.

Indeed, biodiversity has become increasingly mainstreamed into sectoral policies and some of the most significant advances in recent times have been driven by sectors, notably agriculture, water, infrastructure and urban planning. Public awareness of, and involvement in, biodiversity issues is also increasing. Business is now beginning to take heed of biodiversity - often due to corporate social and environmental responsibility but more so through recognition of its role in sustainable and cost-efficient business models.

When it comes to decision-making around biodiversity

issues, there is a broad range of different groups – public and private – that would benefit from being able to take on board ecosystems and ecosystem services more comprehensively. NCA, which will be discussed in more detail in section 3.3 of this paper, is an approach that can help do this. Table 1 in Annex 1 provides examples of these different stakeholders, their biodiversity-related interests and the role NCA can provide for them. For the purposes of this section of the paper, however, examples from business and government will be highlighted. Box 2 below highlights the ever-evolving business case for biodiversity.

photo : Matti Johnson

Box 2: *The evolving business case for biodiversity*

For businesses, their awareness of, and commitment to, biodiversity action still remains fairly limited, despite some forward-thinking motion amongst some companies, which are gradually becoming more informed around biodiversity issues. According to a 2019 OECD report, "a few companies have adopted industry-led commitments (e.g. the 2018 French Act4Nature initiative) and launched various biodiversity initiatives. Financial organizations, on the other hand, are less engaged for biodiversity than businesses, and much less engaged for biodiversity than for climate change" (OECD, 2019b).

At the same time, awareness is undoubtedly growing. According to a recent WEF report, "around USD 44 trillion of economic value generated - more than half of the world's GDP is moderately or highly dependent on nature" (WEF, 2019). This information is now making businesses realize more and more about their dependencies on biodiversity, particularly as they start to appreciate the impact that biodiversity loss will have on their bottom lines. The WEF identified the extractives, construction, energy, fashion and textiles industries being among the sectors especially vulnerable to biodiversity loss and degradation, particularly for their supply chains.

One of the current key challenges for companies is how to measure biodiversity performance, as biodiversity is difficult to capture in one simple metric. However, a number of biodiversity measurement approaches for businesses or financial institutions are available or currently in development. For example, since 2018, the European Union Business & Biodiversity Platform has published annual reports[11] identifying these approaches and providing an independent assessment of the approaches. In the future, the Platform will develop a pragmatic decision tree allowing companies to select the most suitable approach for their specific context.

More broadly speaking, however, a common challenge often faced by policymakers is that different stakeholders have different expectations and interests. For example, widely polarized expectations can prevail in the food sector (TEEB, 2018): the agronomist's primary interest may be feeding the world, the environmentalist's - saving biodiversity, the sociologist's - sustaining rural livelihoods and social equity, the economist's - efficient markets for cheap food, the health specialist's - healthy diets, and the consumer (i.e. voters) may place any combination of these as their priority.

The traditional way of economic accounting for agriculture and other economic activities reliant on nature, is based on a simple production model which does not adequately acknowledge multiple stakeholders. This is partly because traditional economic accounting does not take into consideration the hidden costs of biodiversity loss, nor what and whom this impacts. Only a systems thinking approach - one which enables environment, economic and social considerations to be integrated by including accounting for natural capital stocks and flows - allows for these hidden costs and benefits to be illuminated, and effective policy options and investment choices to be identified.

---

[11] See https://ec.europa.eu/environment/biodiversity/business/news-and-events/news/news-182_en.htm

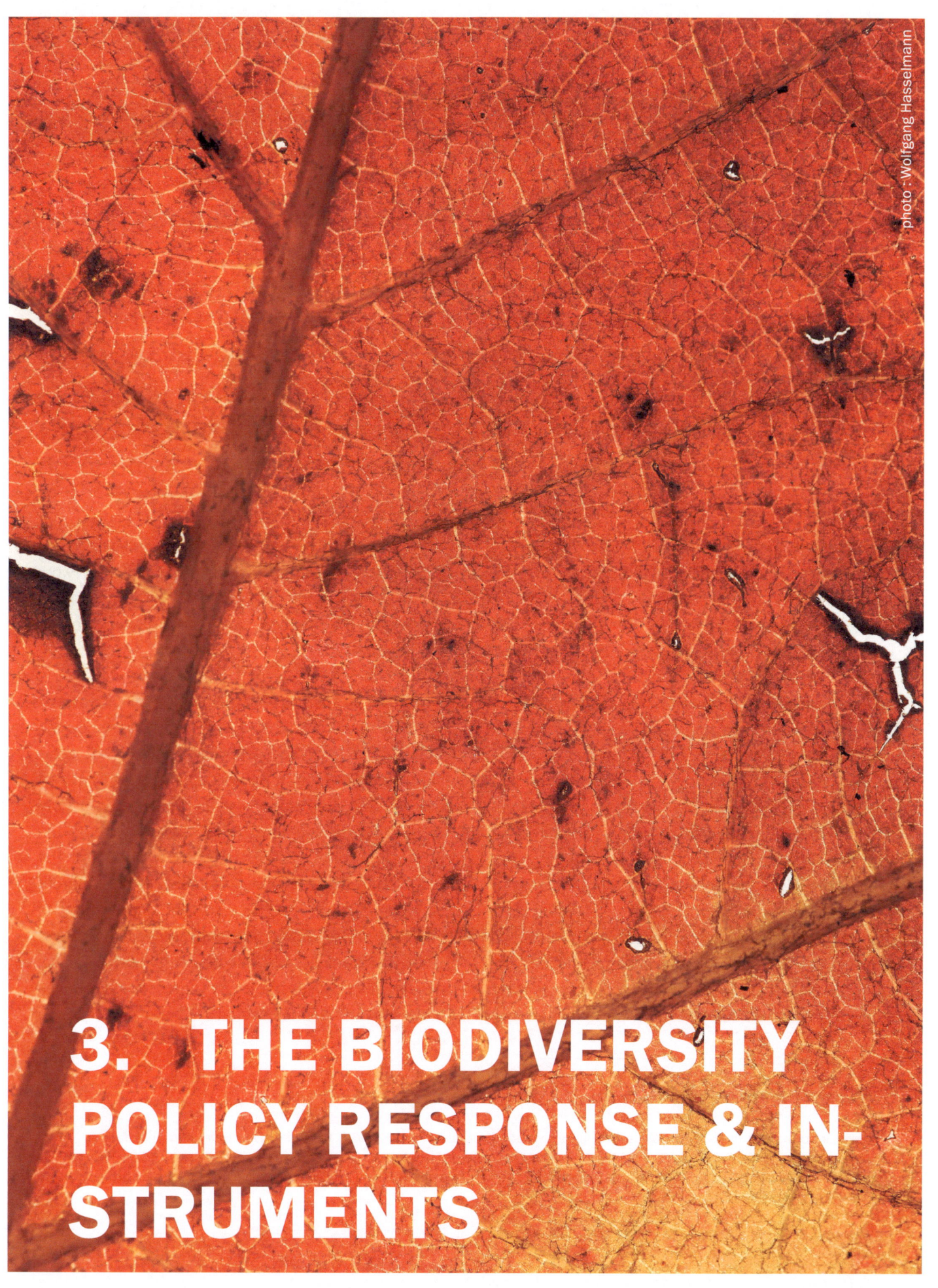

photo · Wolfgang Hasselmann

3.   THE BIODIVERSITY POLICY RESPONSE & INSTRUMENTS

3.1 Existing Frameworks and International Processes

At a general level, there is already consensus that we must better conserve and restore biodiversity if we are to achieve sustainable development, including resource efficient economies, social equity and eliminating poverty. To do this, transformational change is required in how we impact, interact with and manage biodiversity (for example: Leadley et al., 2014; Secretariat of the Convention on Biological Diversity, 2014; United Nations, 2015; IPBES, 2019).

The inter-governmentally agreed overarching policy framework for biodiversity is the Strategic Plan for Biodiversity 2011-2020, adopted by the Convention on Biological Diversity (CBD) in 2010 and accompanied by the 20 Aichi Biodiversity Targets.[12] In most cases, national governments have integrated this plan into national planning, including the identification of national biodiversity targets, which is achieved through national biodiversity strategies and action plans, or equivalent. The UN General Assembly, all of the other biodiversity-related conventions[13], most inter-governmental and non-governmental organizations with a mandate or interest in biodiversity, and many businesses, have adopted this plan and its targets as their guiding framework on biodiversity. As this Strategic Plan and accompanying Aichi Targets are now coming to an end in 2020, the CBD will soon be adopting the post-2020 global biodiversity framework, as a stepping stone towards the 2050 Vision of "Living in harmony with nature".[14] These targets will be updated in the forthcoming post-2020 global biodiversity framework by the Conference of the Parties to the CBD, at the UN Biodiversity Conference in Kunming, China, likely to now be held in 2021.

The 2030 Agenda for Sustainable Development and the SDGs is an overarching, agreed, policy framework, which also encompasses biodiversity. The goals and targets relating to biodiversity (notably Goals 14 and 15, but also references to biodiversity in Goal 2 on food and Goal 6 on water) are aligned with the Strategic Plan for Biodiversity 2011-2020 and the Aichi Biodiversity Targets. Notably, in the current context, SDG Target 15.9 states that countries should aim "by 2020, [to] integrate ecosystem and biodiversity values into national and local planning, development processes, poverty reduction strategies and accounts" and indicator 15.9.1 explicitly refers to

---

[12] See https://www.cbd.int/sp/targets/

[13] In addition to the CBD, these are: the Convention on Conservation of Migratory Species (1979), the Convention on International Trade in Endangered Species of Wild Fauna and Flora (1975), the International Treaty on Plant Genetic Resources for Food and Agriculture (2004), the Ramsar Convention on Wetlands (1971), the World Heritage Convention (1972), the International Plant Protection Convention (1952), and the International Whaling Commission (1946).

[14] See https://www.cbd.int/decision/cop/?id=12268

the mainstreaming of biodiversity values through NCA, specifically implementation of the SEEA. The SDGs cover 17 Goals and 169 targets. These are meant to be achieved collectively and are considered mutually supporting. But teasing out relevant synergies or trade-offs between different goals or targets, for example, achieving food or water security whilst boosting biodiversity outcomes, requires a systems approach, with NCA as an essential tool.

The new decade ahead of us will indeed be an important time for tackling the decline of biodiversity. Beyond the CBD's post-2020 global biodiversity framework, the UN General Assembly made a bold call to action in March 2019 declaring that this next decade will be the UN Decade on Ecosystem Restoration. This "Decade" aims to scale up the restoration of degraded ecosystems as a proven measure to tackle the climate crisis and enhance food security, water supply and biodiversity. According to UN Environment (2019) this call to action "will draw together political support, scientific research and financial muscle to massively scale up restoration from successful pilot initiatives to areas of millions of hectares. Research shows that more than two billion hectares of the world's deforested and degraded landscapes offer potential for restoration". The UN Environment along with FAO will lead the implementation of the Decade with its partners (UN Environment, 2019).

3.2 Policy Instruments

There is no single policy instrument for biodiversity policy - instruments range from protected areas, to community-based resource management, to cultural arrangements and more. The public and private sector put in significant resources into financing biodiversity conservation and protection - a recent estimate puts biodiversity finance to be on the scale of USD 77-87 billion per year (OECD, 2020), though this is arguably not enough to sufficiently safeguard biodiversity.

In the context of NCA, two relevant policy instruments include payment for ecosystem services (PES) and protected areas (PAs). While there are many other relevant policy instruments, PES are elaborated here given their increase in popularity, while PAs are a mainstay of biodiversity conservation.

Over the past several years, there has been a significant rise in the number of PES programmes, under which payments are made for the purpose of undertaking land/ecosystem management practices intended to ensure the delivery of ecosystem services. One of the most well-known PES schemes is the UN Collaborative

---

[15] See https://www.unredd.net/

Programme on Reducing Emissions from Deforestation and Forest Degradation in Developing Countries (REDD+) programme[15], which incentivizes developing countries to contribute to climate change mitigation actions through conservation and sustainable management of forests. However, REDD+ is only one of many programmes. According to a recent estimate, there are over 550 active programmes around the globe which comprise roughly USD 36-42 billion in annual transactions (Salzman et al., 2018). However, the effectiveness of many of these PES schemes is uncertain (Börner et al., 2017; Karousakis, 2018). A lack of sufficient data has been identified as one reason for the lack of rigorous PES scheme evaluations, which are needed to ensure effectiveness (Karousakis, 2018). Thus, in order to create informed PES schemes and carry out more thorough evaluations, governments and others need greater access to rigorous and systematically collected data on ecosystems and the provision of ecosystem services. Natural capital accounts are a key source of data that could improve the evidence base upon which PES are designed and evaluated.

Protected areas (PAs) are another biodiversity policy instrument that has been widely used. They form the cornerstone of biodiversity conservation policy and for good reason. PAs maintain critical habitats for species (often threatened) and ensure the maintenance of natural ecosystem functioning. However, the impact of PAs on human well-being is not always recognized. They provide livelihoods for more than one billion people, provide the primary source of drinking water for over a third of the world's largest cities and help ensure global food security (CBD, 2020). At the same time, many PAs are mismanaged, are situated in areas unimportant for biodiversity, do not abate the threats to their biodiversity nor are they truly managed to promote the long-term conservation of nature (Visconti et al., 2019). Better data that show how PAs are (or are not) delivering biodiversity outcomes is essential in order inform better policy and management (see Box 3).

While well-situated and managed PAs can be very effective at achieving biodiversity outcomes and contributing to human well-being and the economy, countries often struggle to muster the political will to designate more PAs. Case in point - the rate of designation and total extent of additional protected areas between 2010 and 2014, after the establishment of the Aichi Biodiversity Targets, was less than half that in the previous five years (Visconti et al., 2019). However, NCA can help illustrate and make more visible the myriad benefits that protected areas provide - and thus promote their establishment and maintenance.

Box 3: *Understanding the effectiveness of PAs in South Asia*

There is a significant number of PAs in South Asia (Bangladesh, Bhutan, India, Maldives, Nepal, Pakistan and Sri Lanka). In fact, since 1950, South Asia's PA system increased 64-fold. However, there is a poor understanding of how the region's rapidly growing population and economic activity are impacting these PAs. Agricultural conversion, logging, grazing, tourism and many other factors threaten PAs in South Asia. To better understand how effective PAs are in the region, Clark et al. (2013), compared anthropogenic land uses inside and outside South Asia's PA network.

Using multiple land cover datasets to create a time series, they found that each PA had, on average, more than a third of its land cleared for human use, with several sites showing nearly total habitat transformation. In addition, the rates of clearance inside PAs were not found to be statistically different from those outside PAs. Furthermore, the current management regime of the PAs had no significant impact on habitat modification - indicating that there is a pressing need to update management for all PAs (Clark et al., 2013).

Spatially explicit data, such as that compiled by Clark et al., is crucial for understanding where PAs are being degraded. However, this data needs to be systematically collected and standardized in order to inform policies in the longer term. Rigorous and standardized data on the extent to which PA ecosystems are changing, improvements or declines in their condition, and the ecosystem services that are being gained or lost, are all needed in order to understand how to create more effective PA policy in South Asia and beyond.

3.3 The Value of Natural Capital Accounting and the SEEA

As illustrated in section 2, the information requirements surrounding biodiversity policy questions require a large amount of data. Data on ecosystems, and the services that they provide is of vital importance, as is data on species occurrence.

However, data on the drivers of biodiversity loss and degradation are also needed - such as data on pollution and natural resource extraction which are driven by economic activities. Moreover, all of this information and data needs to be consistent and structured in a way that facilitates the creation of integrated policies - policies that connect the environment to the economy. NCA provides a framework to provide such data. Its underlying premise is that since the environment is important to society and the economy, it should be recognized as an asset that must be maintained and managed.

The System of Environmental-Economic Accounting (SEEA) is the accepted international statistical standard for NCA and provides a framework for organizing and presenting statistics on the environment and its relationship with the economy. Placing environmental statistics into an accounting framework dramatically increases their usefulness for policy, enabling international comparability, replication over time, and straightforward integration with existing national accounts. Importantly, the SEEA is well aligned with national accounting principles, namely those used in the System of National Accounts (SNA), from which GDP and other mainstream macroeconomic indicators are derived. This relationship between the SEEA and the SNA allows the SEEA to provide a coherent set of statistics on the environment-economy nexus that can easily be integrated into policy analysis.

The SEEA also fills an important gap in statistics. Headline economic indicators like GDP, provide important information about the state of the economy but omit the crucial role of nature. This means, and to take an extreme but illuminating example, if a country was to cut down all of its forests in a single year, this might show up in official statistics as an increase in GDP due to increased timber production. Such a move, however, would be catastrophic for the country's natural wealth and would likely destroy the forest sector's long-term viability, leading to irreversible environmental damage and enormous long-term social costs. However, by integrating environmental assets and services with data on economic and other human activity, the SEEA expands the perspective and puts nature into the equation.

photo : Osman Rana

4. HOW THE SEEA CAN PROVIDE INFORMATION FOR BIODIVERSITY POLICY

One of the main benefits of the SEEA is that it uses a systems approach to provide a wide range of data, including data on ecosystems and species as well as on drivers of biodiversity loss and policy responses. Thus, users can rely on a single system to understand drivers, impacts, responses, and importantly, the effectiveness of policy responses. The section below briefly outlines the basic concepts of the SEEA and how it relates to biodiversity and then goes on to expand on how it can be used to address some of the policy questions identified in section 2.3.

4.1 The SEEA and Biodiversity

Two different, albeit related, perspectives are embodied in the SEEA - the perspective of individual natural resources and the perspective of ecosystems. The first perspective starts from the viewpoint of the economy and accounts for how natural resources (e.g. water, energy, fish stocks, etc.) are used in production and consumption. It also looks at the resulting impact of this extraction and use of natural resources on the environment (e.g. emissions, depletion of natural resource stocks, etc.) (see Annex 2, Figure 1). This perspective, based on the concept of individual environmental assets, is elaborated in the SEEA Central Framework (SEEA-CF). However, the interactions between the environment and economy go far beyond the extraction and use of natural resources and the resulting pollution and depletion of natural resources. Thus, the SEEA Experimental Ecosystem Accounting (SEEA-EEA) complements the SEEA-CF by considering how individual environmental assets interact as part of natural processes within a given spatial area, i.e. ecosystems.

The primary means by which the SEEA accounts for biodiversity is through the SEEA-EEA, which provides a framework for ecosystem accounting, including four major types of accounts: 1) ecosystem extent, or the size and occurrence of ecosystems; 2) condition, or the health of ecosystems; 3) ecosystem services, or the contributions of ecosystems to benefits used in economic and other human activity; and 4) asset accounts, which record the monetary value of opening and closing stocks of all ecosystems. A notable aspect of the SEEA-EEA is that it is spatially explicit, allowing the presentation of the accounts through maps. This means that ecosystems, their condition and the services they provide can be mapped over time, allowing users to identify where and when changes are occurring. It should also be noted that the SEEA-EEA can be in both biophysical and monetary terms. The main focus of ecosystem accounting is the supply of final ecosystem services to economic units (e.g. businesses, households, etc.), and this information can be supplied in both physical and monetary terms.

While the SEEA-EEA accounts for biodiversity mainly at the ecosystem level, it also includes information on biodiversity at the level of species through dedicated species accounts. These species-occurrence accounts can be used for species conservation and monitoring and also as an indicator for ecosystem condition. A fully-fledged accounting system at the species level (analogous in scope to the current SEEA-EEA) is currently being investigated. In addition, while SEEA-EEA does not currently contain information on genetic diversity, how the SEEA-EEA can address this in the future is also currently being examined (see Section 4.6).

The SEEA-CF is also relevant to biodiversity policy on ecosystems. In particular, the SEEA-CF contains environmental activity accounts, which provide information on transactions concerning activity undertaken to preserve and protect the environment, including those for biodiversity protection. Thus, the SEEA-CF provides valuable information on the policy responses, which, when used in conjunction with SEEA-EEA accounts, shows the effectiveness of these policy responses. Annex 2 provides further details on the SEEA and its analytical applications.

The SEEA can be an extremely powerful and helpful tool when it comes to formulating policies designed at addressing the drivers of biodiversity loss and degradation, as specified in Section 2. Three of the key drivers that the next sections will now look at, using a series of examples, are land use change, climate change and pollution. Whilst the interconnectedness of these challenges/policy questions needs to be observed, their differences and separate importance allow for standalone discussions where the appropriate connections between them can also be made.

photo : JF Brou

4.2   How the SEEA can Address Land Use Change Drivers

Many of the major policy questions linked to land use change (section 2.3.1) surround a need to better understand the trade-offs involved.

For example, should a forest be preserved for recreation and carbon sequestration, or be logged to generate income and raw material? While logging can provide economic benefits, what consequences does this have for overall ecosystem health? And at what point do such activities threaten ecosystem resilience?

In order to answer such questions, policymakers would need rigorous, standardized data on land use and ecosystems, including an understanding of who the beneficiaries are of the ecosystem services provided by forests - which range from timber provisioning to carbon sequestration to recreation to soil retention and more. The SEEA-EEA provides a comprehensive set of accounts on ecosystems and their contribution to the economy which allows policymakers to access the data they need to make more informed decisions moving forward.

For instance, ecosystem extent accounts can show the extent and location of forest ecosystems through maps, which can be linked to data on land use, management and ownership. The damage caused by logging and any restoration efforts by logging companies can be shown through ecosystem condition accounts and maps. Finally, ecosystem service accounts track the services provided by forests and who uses these services. Thus, ecosystem service accounts would show how much the forestry sector gains by logging the forest - and how this links to diminished carbon sequestration over time. However, forests are only one of many types of ecosystems which face competing uses. Box 4 below illustrates the SEEA in action and how it has informed competing interests and priorities in the Netherlands, when it comes to peatlands.

Box 4: *Managing peatlands in the Netherlands*

Consisting of plant remains (about 10 per cent by weight of peat) and water (90 per cent), peatlands are considered to be one of the most challenging ecosystems on the planet to manage. Not only do their swampy conditions make access difficult, but their high water table prevents the cultivation of most crops. This means that drainage is essential in order to use them productively for cultivation. However, and whilst drainage allows for agricultural activities on peatlands, it also exposes the organic matter in the soil to oxygen in the atmosphere. The oxidation of organic matter leads to CO_2 emissions, and drainage also leads to sunken grounds which leave the drained peatlands vulnerable to floods.

In the Netherlands, peatlands cover around 8 per cent of the land area and are mainly used for dairy farming. Among farmers, there is a tendency to prefer lower water tables which not only allows for easier access to the meadows but also favours the growth of grass. The resulting national CO_2 emissions, caused by the drainage, are around 6 to 7 million tonnes CO_2 per year (some 4 per cent of the national total CO_2 emissions). Their management has multiple dimensions, ranging from generational farming, to income dependency for farming peatlands, to a reliance by some of the food processing industry, who are dependent upon the milk produced. This means that farmers can be reluctant to acknowledge the externalities of peatland drainage, which not only include CO_2 emissions but also the maintenance of infrastructure (roads, dykes, sewage systems) affected by continuous soil subsidence in drained peatlands, among others. In all, these externalities have been estimated to amount to up to 1000-1500 euro per hectare of drained farmland per year.

Unfortunately, there is no technical solution to the problem that allows farmers to drain the peatlands without producing significant externalities. Therefore, trade-offs in landscape management are unavoidable. Government intervention can reduce the externalities placed upon society, but at the expense of farmers' income.

Decision-making on the use of natural resources usually involves balancing diverging interests and considering social, environmental and economic dimensions of different options. At the time the Dutch SEEA-EEA accounts were published, a broad stakeholder engagement had been started by the Dutch government to discuss climate change targets and measures to be taken to reach these sectors. Peat management featured prominently in the discussion on how the agricultural sector could reduce GHG emissions. The Netherlands carbon account was published just prior to the start of these negotiations. The account showed clearly the contribution of peatlands to national CO_2 emissions. It also showed that, at a micro-level, profits from farming were smaller than the monetized costs of CO_2 emissions and resulting damages. As a result, in the final, agreed sectoral climate change mitigation plan, the focus shifted towards taking land out of production and increasing water levels to the surface to avoid all CO_2 emissions in these areas, while at the same time further testing technical approaches at pilot scale. An amount of 250 million euros has been reserved for converting drained farmland to undrained land, including for use as nature areas and no-drainage agriculture (Government of the Netherlands, 2019). Furthermore, an initial law has been proposed to further support and incentivize farmers to stop farming in peatlands (Bromet and De Groot, 2019).

Carbon account map for the Netherlands, showing carbon emissions from peatland drainage
(source map: SEEA Carbon Account published by Statistics the Netherlands and Wageningen University, 2017)

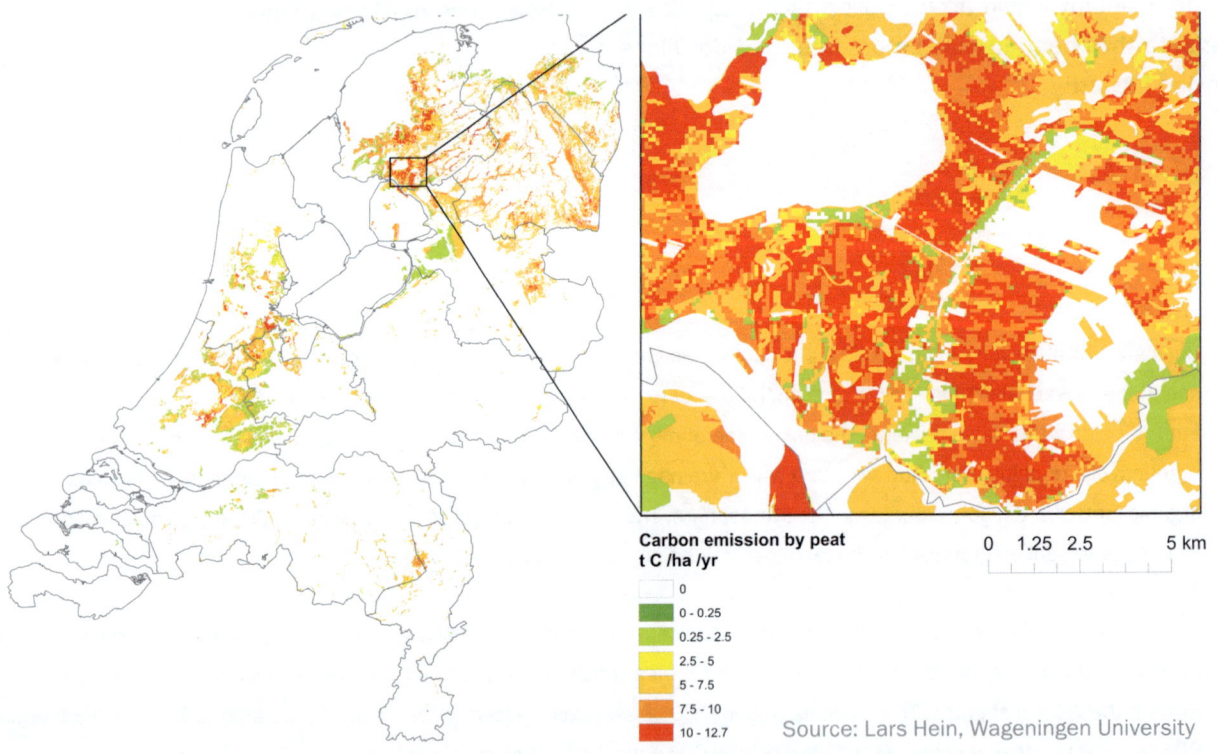

Source: Lars Hein, Wageningen University

4.3 How the SEEA can Address Climate Change Drivers

Other major biodiversity policy questions are linked to climate change challenges (section 2.3.2), particularly considering how vulnerable ecosystems and the provision of vital ecosystem services are to climate change impacts. Even small changes in average temperature can have a significant effect upon ecosystem functioning and condition.

Already the climate change impacts of today are affecting the habitats of countless species, for example. Given the urgency of the climate problem, both climate change mitigation and adaptation need to be tackled head-on. Thus, policymakers face a two-fold question. In terms of mitigation, policymakers need to identify the economic drivers of emissions and in terms of adaptation, they need to understand what the impacts of climate change are, and where they are occurring.

By utilising SEEA accounts, policymakers can address both climate change mitigation and adaptation. When it comes to climate mitigation, policymakers are turning more and more to footprints (for example, carbon footprints) to understand the emission impacts of production. Carbon footprints derived from the SEEA-CF can identify the amount of CO_2 emitted to produce a final product, including emissions from intermediate inputs and emissions embedded in imported intermediate and final products. This important analytical tool can be used to understand which product- and consumption-related policies can help limit CO_2 emissions.

For climate adaptation, the SEEA-EEA can pinpoint the impacts of climate change on ecosystems and ecosystem services. Since the accounts are spatially explicit and are meant to be compiled over time, users can identify for example, changes in ecosystem extent and condition over time. This is especially important for ecosystems vulnerable to climate change, such as forests and alpine areas, and ecosystem service accounts show where and how climate change is impacting critical ecosystem services. Furthermore, ecosystem service accounts also show which ecosystems are delivering services to help deal with the impacts of climate change, for example through flood mitigation. Information on both these aspects of climate change adaptation can enable informed and effective adaptation strategies.

The use of the accounts for climate change adaptation is shown in the below example for Rwanda (Box 5). This example shows the importance of creating policies that consider biodiversity and climate change together. It further demonstrates how the spatially explicit nature of the accounts facilitates policymaking at all scales - from local to global levels.

photo : Taylor Deas-Melesh

Box 5: *Rwanda and SEEA-EEA water accounts*

Concern over the impacts of climate change has been one of the motivations to start SEEA Experimental Ecosystem Accounting in Rwanda, under the World Bank Wealth Accounting and Valuation of Ecosystem Services (WAVES Programme) and its successor, the Global Program for Sustainability (GPS). While Rwanda has been endowed with abundant freshwater resources, water supply is becoming more variable and droughts and floods more common. Thus, with support from the World Bank WAVES/GPS, the Government of Rwanda compiled water and ecosystem accounts with an eye to developing more resilient catchments that can withstand the effects of climate change. Over the last 25 years, increasingly erratic and seasonally fluctuating river levels have meant that the amount of fast flowing and destructive water flows (quick flow) has increased by 35 per cent. Rivers are no longer able to meet a consumer demand throughout the year and Rwanda faces increased risks and costs of flooding (see map below).

Rwanda's spatially explicit water accounts are key to identifying and monitoring high-yield catchments vulnerable to flooding and land-slides. Since Rwanda has limited opportunities to influence global climate change impacts, the development of resilient catchments that are able to withstand both global shocks and greater local pressures is a vital climate change adaptation strategy which will have important benefits for biodiversity.

Map of Rwanda showing annual water yield in 2015:
High water yields are associated with greater quick flow and flooding risks.

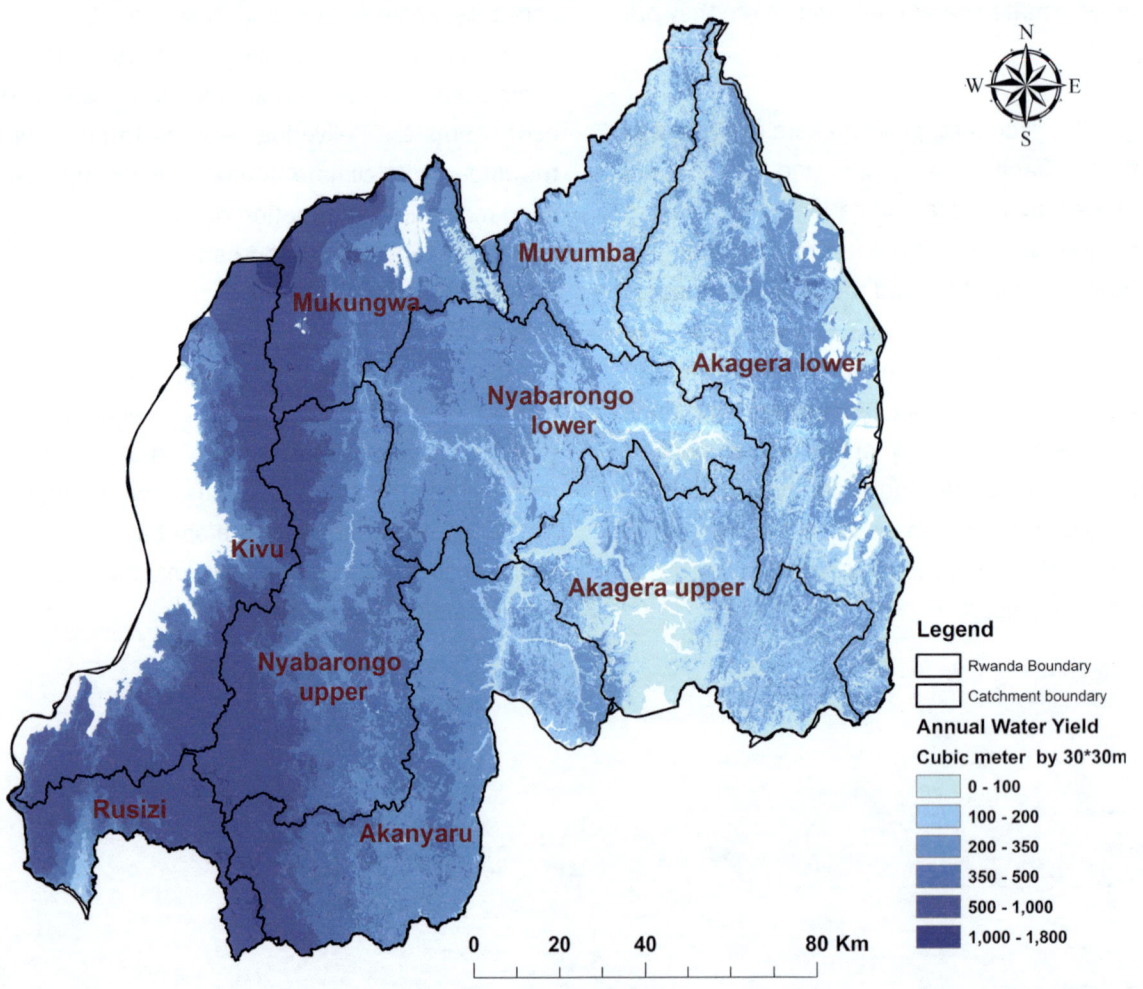

Source: Government of Rwanda, 2019

4.4 How the SEEA can Address Pollution Drivers

Other key biodiversity policy questions are those connected to air and water pollution (section 2.3.4) such as greenhouse gas emissions, untreated waste and oil spills as well as marine plastics, to name but a few. The policy issues here, and particularly where SEEA could be of use, concern identifying the costs of pollution and specifically helping to understand at what point the costs arising from the economic activities behind pollution start to outweigh the benefits.

Furthermore, the SEEA can also be used to understand how biodiversity and ecosystem services can provide solutions for pollution.

The impact of pollution on ecosystems and ecosystem services can be shown through SEEA-EEA accounts. In particular, ecosystem condition accounts can be used to illustrate the health of ecosystems and inform the capacity of ecosystems to provide vital ecosystem services. The spatially explicit nature of ecosystem accounts further informs ecosystem rehabilitation and management policies. This is illustrated below in Box 6, which details South Africa's river extent and condition accounts and how they can inform policy. At the same time, it is important to note that the SEEA can also help identify and evaluate solutions to combat pollution. For instance, SEEA-EEA accounts can also provide

information on the effectiveness of nature based solutions, such as protecting or restoring ecosystems, through ecosystem service accounts for water and air filtration services.

In addition, the SEEA-CF can provide policymakers with information needed to address the indirect economic drivers of pollution. Several SEEA-CF accounts provide information on the air and water pollution, and importantly, can be used to understand the consumer demand behind the production activities causing this pollution. For example, air emission accounts in the SEEA-CF can be used to disaggregate air emissions by the specific industries responsible as well as attribute emissions to categories of products and services. This allows policymakers to understand how they can best structure their air emission regulations.

photo : Hasan Almasi

Box 6: *The SEEA and Biodiversity in South Africa*

Rivers are critically important ecosystems in South Africa, not only for water supply, but for agriculture and energy as well. They are also incredibly numerous in South Africa. In fact, the total length of all of South Africa's rivers would encircle the globe four times (Statistics South Africa, 2017). To ensure that rivers are healthy enough to continue to provide drinking water, water for agriculture and feed into dams, Statistics South Africa and the South African National Biodiversity Institute (SANBI) have worked together to compile national river ecosystem extent and condition accounts.

Condition accounts were chosen in part because pollution from mining, cultivation, irrigation, sewage and other activities have had important repercussions for the health of South Africa's rivers. Thus, the condition accounts included a water quality indicator that measured the water quality modification based on direct water quality data and expert knowledge on pollution from point/non-point sources. Additional indicators in the condition accounts included flow, in-stream habitat and stream bank/riparian habitat indicators.

As the SEEA framework can provide a basis for aggregate indicators, Statistics South Africa and SANBI used the condition account to calculate an aggregated, easily interpretable ecological condition index. By highlighting the degree to which rivers have been modified by human activity, the accounts provide vital information on the impact human activity has had in terms of ecosystem degradation. Strikingly, the study found that there was an overall 10 per cent decline in ecological condition of rivers from between 1999 to 2011. The accounts also identified the areas where the decline in river health has been most pronounced, so that solutions can be identified and targeted to better manage catchments and rivers to support economic and social development. By presenting the accounts in biophysical, as well as administrative units, they can serve as a measurement framework for monitoring Water Management Areas in South Africa and are helping to inform the National Water and Sanitation Master Plan that is currently being developed by the Department of Water and Sanitation (Nel and Driver, 2015).

Map of the aggregated ecological condition category for main rivers in South Africa, 1999 and 2011.

Main rivers (1999)   Main rivers (2011)

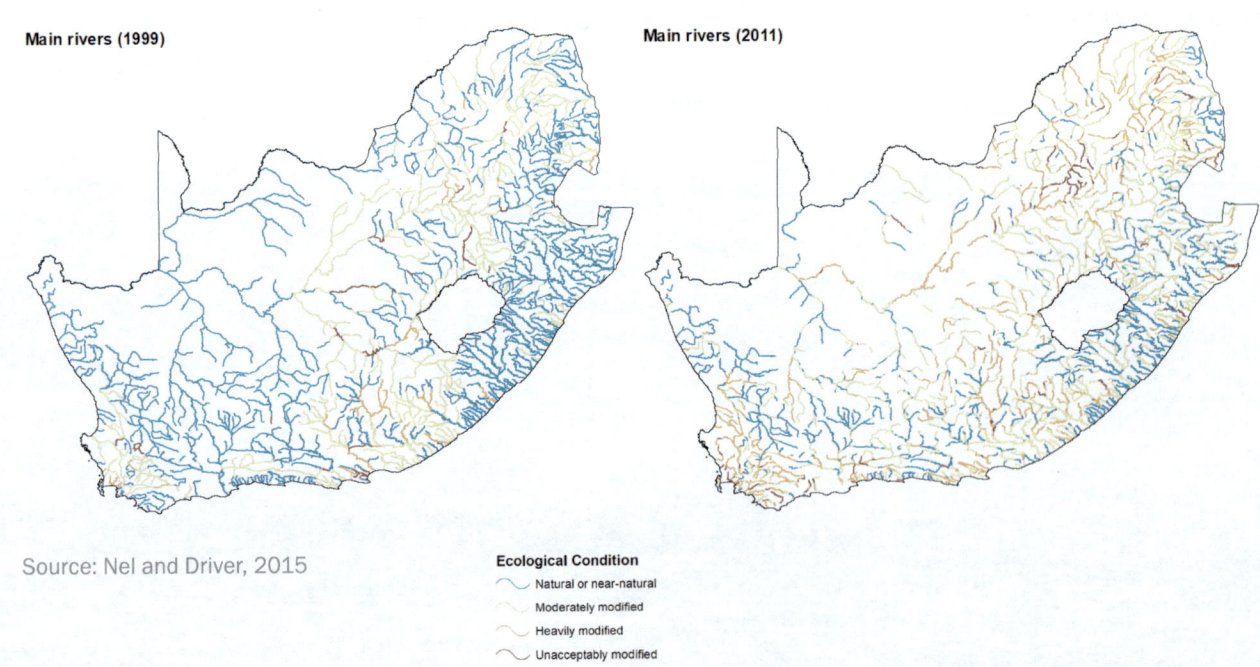

Source: Nel and Driver, 2015

Ecological Condition
- Natural or near-natural
- Moderately modified
- Heavily modified
- Unacceptably modified

4.5 Complementing Ongoing International Initiatives Surrounding Biodiversity

A key aspect of achieving the goals of the upcoming post-2020 global biodiversity framework is the ability of countries to effectively and sustainably monitor progress towards meeting defined targets. There is broad acknowledgement that there has not been enough progress towards the Aichi targets under the Strategic Plan for Biodiversity 2011-2020 (IPBES, 2019). However, given the current state of biodiversity, there is little room to make the same mistakes again.

One of the reasons put forward behind the lack of success is that the format of the targets made progress difficult to measure and the targets themselves were not realistic. In particular, a study by Green et al. (2019) found that there was a positive relationship between progress and the extent to which the target elements were perceived to be measurable, realistic, unambiguous and scalable. Some have argued further that the Aichi targets also failed to meet expectations because countries were not held accountable to report what they were doing to achieve the targets (Nature, 2020).

Thus, the SEEA can play a role in two ways. The first is to serve as a standardized, rigorous monitoring framework for the agreed targets and indicators of the post-2020 global biodiversity framework. Given the scope of the SEEA and its ability to address drivers and impacts, it is well placed to serve as a coherent and effective measurement framework. A preliminary analysis by the United Nations Statistics Division indicates that the SEEA can be used as a measurement framework for 27 of 45 of the draft indicators for the 2050 Goals and 60 out of 147 of the indicators for 2030 Goals proposed in the preliminary draft monitoring framework. The second way the SEEA can contribute is as a reporting framework. As noted in a recent editorial in Nature (2020), national statistical offices are well posed to report on progress towards the post-2020 global biodiversity framework. Given their independence, knowledge of the SEEA and ability to adhere to strict deadlines, national statistical offices can greatly contribute to reporting by providing high-quality official statistics and by coordinating reporting efforts by various ministries.

In addition, this decade ahead of us is the UN Decade on Ecosystem Restoration. Here, too, the SEEA can play a valuable role in serving as the measurement framework to track progress towards restoring degraded ecosystems. Not only can the SEEA-EEA provide the means to monitor ecosystem extent, condition and services, but the SEEA-CF also provides a means to track expenditures on protection of biodiversity, landscapes, species and habitats. Used in conjunction, the SEEA-CF and SEEA-EEA can help monitor the effectiveness of actions taken under the initiative.

4.6 Moving Forward: Improving the Integration of Biodiversity into the SEEA

Biodiversity, particularly at the level of ecosystems, is already at the core of the SEEA-EEA. However, the UN Committee of Experts on Environmental-Economic Accounting[16] (UNCEEA) is currently revising the SEEA-EEA and refining how biodiversity is reflected. Areas of work include:

- **Accounting for non-tangible benefits and flows:** The SEEA-EEA does not deal with all aspects of biodiversity, notably, regarding non-tangible (non-quantifiable) biodiversity benefits such as "existence value", "intrinsic value" and "religious and cultural values". However, under the revision of the SEEA-EEA, the UNCEEA is examining how the SEEA-EEA fits into this wider range of values and can complement other frameworks.

- **Accounting for species- and genetic-level diversity:** Although the SEEA already contains species accounts, there is a need to move beyond the species abundance accounts that are currently captured in the SEEA-EEA, and design species accounts that better reflect a systemic view. In addition, the SEEA does not currently account for genetic diveristy. Thus, efforts to develop a full methodology for species and genetic accounts are currently being undertaken. Finally, no single component of biodiversity (ecosystems, species and genes) can provide ecosystem services alone. More work needs to be done to understand how the three components of biodiveristy interact to provide ecosystem services, and how this can be reflected in the SEEA.

- **Accounting for resilience:** One of the most important aspects of biodiversity is how it underpins ecosystem resilience. More biodiverse ecosystems tend to be more resilient to change. This is partly because the more species there are, the more ecological options there are to respond to change. This tends to reduce the chances of ecosystem collapse or failure. However, at present, resilience is not well elaborated in the SEEA. A number of measurable ecosystem services are related directly to increasing resilience or reducing risk, or accounting for biodiversity in the context of future value, insurance and risk: for example, those related to disaster risk reduction. In a similar vein, "tipping points" (beyond which ecosystems collapse, or undergo rapid irreversible change into a different condition) can be difficult to identify and, therefore, account for. Tipping points can rarely be accurately identified, but when they are, they can be factored into accounting, ensuring that policies are in place to prevent overshooting this tipping point.

---

[16] The UN Committee of Experts on Environmental-Economic Accounting (UNCEEA) was established by the UN Statistical Commission at its 36th session in March 2005. The UNCEEA provides overall vision, coordination, prioritization and direction in the field of environmental economic accounting and supporting statistics.

5. CONCLUSIONS

photo . O . A . P...

Despite the overwhelmingly negative trend in biodiversity loss, this trend can be stopped, and possibly reversed. However, such transformative change will require new approaches, data systems and policies.

There is growing recognition of the need for systems thinking that understands the role of ecosystems and ecosystem services in sustainable economies, with NCA as a critical tool to help identify better policy outcomes.

Accounting for biodiversity will be an essential part of identifying pathways to sustainability and realigning the environment and economy to be mutually supporting. Together, the SEEA-EEA and the SEEA-CF provide an effective and comprehensive approach towards providing the data needed for effective policies, and further developments of the SEEA-EEA in terms of species and genetic diversity will enhance the relevance of the accounts. Furthermore, the application of the SEEA can also assist in the operationalizing, costing and mainstreaming of national biodiversity strategies and action plans across economic and financing policy arenas.

The experience to date indicates that there are some key policy areas that biodiversity accounting can address (UNCEEA, 2018). Some of the clearest applications relate to land use management and prioritizing conservation areas. But perhaps more importantly, in several countries the accounts have influenced policymaking by demonstrating the importance of biodiversity to economic activity and hence elevating its importance in the policy agenda.

SEEA accounts can draw together information that can help achieve National Biodiversity Strategies and Action Plans, the post-2020 global biodiversity framework, biodiversity-related SDGs, national development planning and land use planning. Nearly 100 countries have compiled SEEA accounts, and as SEEA implementation spreads even further, biodiversity will enter the mainstream of government decision-making. This gives biodiversity the chance of being effectively conserved, restored and used sustainably, while simultaneously meeting other global societal goals (IPBES, 2019). Indeed, the SDGs and the 2050 Vision for Biodiversity can be achieved with transformative change, the conditions for which can put in place now.

REFERENCES

photo : Jon

Börner, J., Baylis, K., Corbera, E., Ezzine-de-Blas, D., Honey-Rosés, J., Persson, U.M. and Wunder, S. (2017). The Effectiveness of Payments for Environmental Services. *World Development* (96), 359-374.

Bromet, L. and de Groot, T. (2019). Initiative for new regulations on climate and nature in Netherlands. https://www.parlementairemonitor.nl/9353000/1/j9vvij5epmj1ey0/vkvyko31yzzx. Accessed 20 April 2020.

Convention on Biological Diversity (CBD) (2010). About Climate Change and Biodiversity. https://www.cbd.int/climate/intro.shtml. Accessed 20 April 2020.

CBD (2014). Global Biodiversity Outlook 4. Montréal. 155pp.

CBD (2020). Protected Areas – an overview. https://www.cbd.int/protected/overview/. Accessed March 2020.

Clark, N.E., Boakes, E.H., McGowan, P.J.K., Mace, G.M. and Fuller, R.A. (2013). Protected Areas in South Asia Have Not Prevented Habitat Loss: A Study Using Historical Models of Land use Change. *PLoS ONE* 8(5): e65298.

Costanza, R., de Groot, R.S. Sutton, P., van der Ploeg, S., Anderson, S.J., Kubiszewski, I., Farber, S., and Turner, R.K. (2014). Changes in the Global Value of Ecosystem Services. *Global Environmental Change* 26 (May 2014): 152–58. https://www. sciencedirect.com/science/article/abs/pii/ S0959378014000685.

Food and Agriculture Organization of the United Nations (FAO) (2019). The State of the World's Biodiversity for Food and Agriculture. J. Bélanger & D. Pilling (eds.). FAO Commission on Genetic Resources for Food and Agriculture Assessments. Rome. 572 pp. http://www.fao.org/3/CA3129EN/CA3129EN.pdf. Accessed 20 April 2020.

Government of the Netherlands (2019). Climate Agreement. The Hague. https://www.government.nl/documents/reports/2019/06/28/climate-agreement. Accessed 29 April 2020.

Government of Rwanda (2019). Rwanda Natural Capital Accounts – Ecosystems. Kigali. https://www. wavespartnership.org/sites/waves/files/kc/Rwandaper cent20NCAper cent20Ecosystemper cent20Accountsper cent20_Publishedper cent20onper cent203-12-2019.pdf. Accessed 20 April 2020.

Green, E.J., Buchanan, G., Butchart, S.H.M., Chandler, G.M., Burgess, N.D., Hill, S.L.L. and Gregory, R.D. (2019). Relating characteristics of global biodiversity targets to reported progress. *Conservation Biology* 33(6), 1360-1369.

Hanssen, F., Barton, D.N., Nowell, M., and Cimburova, Z. (2019). Mapping urban tree canopy cover using airborne laser scanning – applications to urban ecosystem accounting for Oslo. *NINA Report* 1677. Oslo: Norwegian Institute for Nature Research.

Hein, L., Bagstad, K.J., Obst, C., Edens, B., Schenau, S., Castillo, G., Soulard, F., Brown, C., Driver, A., Bordt, M., Steurer, A., Harris, R. and Caparrós, A. (2020). Progress in natural capital accounting for ecosystems. *Science* 367, 514.

Intergovernmental Science-Policy Platform on Biodiversity and Ecosystem Services (IPBES) (2019). Summary for policymakers of the global assessment report on biodiversity and ecosystem services of the Intergovernmental

Science-Policy Platform on Biodiversity and Ecosystem Services. Díaz, S., Settele, J., Brondizio, E. S., Ngo, H. T., Guèze, M., Agard, J., Arneth, A., Balvanera, P., Brauman, K. A., Butchart, S. H. M., Chan, K. M. A., Garibaldi, L. A., Ichii, K., Liu, J., Subramanian, S. M., Midgley, G. F., Miloslavich, P., Molnár, Z., Obura, D., Pfaff, A., Polasky, S., Purvis, A., Razzaque, J., Reyers, B., Roy Chowdhury, R., Shin, Y. J., Visseren-Hamakers, I. J., Willis, K. J. and Zayas, C. N. (eds.). IPBES secretariat, Bonn, Germany. In press.

Intergovernmental Panel on Climate Change (IPCC) (2018). Summary for Policymakers. In: Global Warming of 1.5°C. An IPCC Special Report on the impacts of global warming of 1.5°C above pre-industrial levels and related global greenhouse gas emission pathways, in the context of strengthening the global response to the threat of climate change, sustainable development, and efforts to eradicate poverty. Masson-Delmotte, V., Zhai, P., Pörtner, H.O., Roberts, D., Skea, J., Shukla, P.R., Pirani, A., Moufouma-Okia, W., Péan, C., Pidcock, R., Connors, S. Matthews, J.B.R., Chen, Y., Zhou, X., Gomis, M.I., Lonnoy, E., Maycock, T., Tignor, M. and Waterfield, T. (eds.). In Press.

Intergovernmental Panel on Climate Change (IPCC) (2019). Summary for Policymakers. In: Climate Change and Land: an IPCC special report on climate change, desertification, land degradation, sustainable land management, food security, and greenhouse gas fluxes in terrestrial ecosystems. Shukla, P.R., Skea, J., Buendia, E.C., Masson-Delmotte, V., Pörtner, H.-O., Roberts, D.C., Zhai, P., Slade, R., Connors, S., van Diemen, R., Ferrat, M., Haughey, E., Luz, S., Neogi, S., Pathak, M., Petzold, J., Portugal Pereira, J., Vyas, P., Huntley, E., Kissick, K., Belkacemi, M., and Malley, J. (eds.). In press.

International Union for Conservation of Nature (IUCN) (2017). Forests and Climate Change. Issues Brief. https://www.iucn.org/sites/dev/files/forests_and_climate_change_issues_brief.pdf. Accessed 20 April 2020.

Karousakis, K. (2018). Evaluating the effectiveness of policy instruments for biodiversity: Impact evaluation, cost-effectiveness analysis and other approaches. *OECD Environment Working Papers* 141. Paris: Organisation for Economic Co-operation and Development.

King, S., Brown, C., Harfoot, M., and Wilson, L. (2016). Exploring approaches for Constructing Species Accounts in the Context of the SEEA-EEA. Cambridge: United Nations Environment Programme-World Conservation Monitoring Centre.

Leadley, P.W., Krug, C.B., Alkemade, R., Pereira, H.M., Sumaila U.R., Walpole, M., Marques, A., Newbold, T., Teh, L.S.L, van Kolck, J., Bellard, C., Januchowski-Hartley, S.R. and Mumby, P.J. (2014). Progress towards the Aichi Biodiversity Targets: An Assessment of Biodiversity Trends, Policy Scenarios and Key Actions. *Technical Series* 78, 500 pages. Montreal: Secretariat of the Convention on Biological Diversity.

Mori, A.S., Furukawa, T., and Sasaki, T. (2013). Response diversity determines the resilience of ecosystems to environmental change. *Biological Reviews* 88(2), 349–364.

Nature (2020). The United Nations must get its new biodiversity targets right. *Nature* 578, 337-338.

Nel, J. L. and Driver, A. (2015). National river ecosystem accounts for South Africa: Discussion document. http://www.statssa.gov.za/wp-content/uploads/2016/08/National-River-Ecosystem-Accounts-Discussion-Document-FINAL.pdf. Accessed 20 April 2020.

Organisation for Economic Co-operation and Development (OECD) (2015). Table 1: Net Official Development Assistance from DAC and Other Donors in 2014. www.oecd.org/dac/stats/documentupload/ODAper cent202014per cent20Tablesper cent20andper cent20Charts.pdf. Accessed 20 April 2020.

OECD (2016). The economic consequences of outdoor air pollution. Policy Highlights.

https://www.oecd.org/environment/indicators-modelling-outlooks/Policy-Highlights-Economic-consequences-of-outdoor-air-pollution-web.pdf. Accessed 20 April 2020.

OECD (2019a). Statistics Newsletter. December 2019, Issue 71.

OECD (2019b). Biodiversity: Finance and the Economic and Business Case for Action. Report prepared for the G7 Environment Ministers Meeting, 5-6 May 2019.

OECD (2020). A Comprehensive Overview of Global Biodiversity Finance: Initial results. Thematic Workshop on Resource Mobilisation for the Post-2020 Global Biodiversity Framework, January 14-16 2020. https://www.oecd.org/environment/resources/biodiversity/report-a-comprehensive-overview-of-global-biodiversity-finance.pdf. Accessed 20 April 2020.

Pascual, U., Balvanera, P and Díaz, S. (2017). Valuing nature's contributions to people: the IPBES approach. *Current Opinion in Environmental Sustainability*, 26-27 (June 2017): 7-16.

Salzman, J., Bennet, G., Carroll, N., Goldstein, A. and Jenkins, M. (2018). The global status and trends of Payments for Ecosystem Services. *Nature Sustainability* 1, 136-144.

Spurgeon, J., Obst, C., Santamaria, M., Gough, M. and Spencer, R. (2018). Combining Forces: Priority Areas for Collaboration: A Thought Leadership Paper on Advancing Natural Capital Approaches. James Spurgeon (Sustain Value), Carl Obst (IDEEA Group), Marta Santamaria (Natural Capital Coalition), Mark Gough (Natural Capital Coalition) and Richard Spencer (ICAEW).

Statistics South Africa (2017). Four facts about our rivers you probably didn't know. 2 February 2017. http://www.statssa.gov.za/?p=9490. Accessed April 2020.

The Economics of Ecosystems and Biodiversity (TEEB) (2011). The Economics of Ecosystems and Biodiversity in National and International Policy Making. Edited by Patrick ten Brink. London and Washington: Earthscan.

TEEB (2018). TEEB for Agriculture & Food: Scientific and Economic Foundations. Geneva: UN Environment.

The Guardian (2018). Thailand bay made famous by The Beach closed indefinitely. https://www.theguardian.com/world/2018/oct/03/thailand-bay-made-famous-by-the-beach-closed-indefinitely. Accessed 20 April 2020.

United Nations Committee of Experts on Environmental-Economic Accounting (UNCEEA) (2018). The Role of the System of Environmental- Economic Accounting as a Measurement Framework in Support of the post-2020 Agenda. New York: United Nations.

UN Environment (2019). New UN Decade on Ecosystem Restoration offers unparalleled opportunity for job creation, food security and addressing climate change. https://www.unenvironment.org/news-and-stories/press-release/new-un-decade-ecosystem-restoration-offers-unparalleled-opportunity. Accessed 20 April 2020.

United Nations, European Union, Food and Agriculture Organization of the United Nations, International Monetary Fund, Organisation for Economic Co-operation and Development and the World Bank (2014a). System of Environmental-Economic Accounting 2012--Central Framework. New York. ST/ESA/STAT/Ser.F/109

United Nations, European Union, Food and Agriculture Organization of the United Nations, Organisation for Economic Co-operation and Development and World Bank Group (2014b). System of Environmental-Economic Accounting 2012 Experimental Ecosystem Accounting. New York. ST/ESA/STAT/Ser.F/112

United Nations (2015). Transforming our World: the 2030 Agenda for Sustainable Development. Resolution 70/1 of the United Nations General Assembly.

Visconti, P., Marnewick, D., Brooks, T., and Yanosky, A.A. (2019). Protected area targets post-2020. *Science* 364(6437), 239-241.

World Economic Forum (WEF) (2019). The Global Risks Report 2019, 14th Edition. World Economic Forum.

World Health Organization (WHO) Regional Office for Europe & OECD (2015). Economic cost of the health impact of air pollution in Europe: Clean air, health and wealth. Copenhagen.

WHO Regional Office for Europe (2017). Urban Green Spaces: A Brief for Action. http://www.euro.who.int/__data/assets/pdf_file/0010/342289/Urban-Green-Spaces_EN_WHO_web3.pdf?ua=1. Accessed 31 March 2020.

photo : David Clode

ANNEXES

ANNEX 1: EXAMPLES OF DIFFERENT STAKEHOLDERS, THEIR BIODIVERSITY-RELATED INTERESTS AND THE ROLE NCA CAN PROVIDE FOR THEM

TABLE 1

POLICY-MAKER/ USER GROUP	BIODIVERSITY-RELATED INTERESTS	AGENCIES/INSTITUTIONS/ PERSONNEL	ROLE OF NATURAL CAPITAL ACCOUNTING IN IDENTIFYING:
Lawmakers	Biodiversity-related legislation	Parliamentarians, senates, congress, local councils etc.	Aligned biodiversity-related law/regulations to reflect governmental/societal policy objectives Coherence between local, national, regional and global legal/regulatory instruments and obligations
GOVERNMENT AGENCIES:			
Environment	Achieving biodiversity-related objectives (e.g. biodiversity conservation targets) Environmental sustainability	Environment and/or natural resources ministries and departments	Drafting and implementing biodiversity related regulations Biodiversity responses (e.g. protected areas) Liaison with other interests on biodiversity related policy goals Convening stakeholders
Finance/planning/ economics	Effective budget allocations meeting multiple goals Economic efficiency and resources allocation	Finance ministry/department and or national planning authority	Oversight of government department budgets Financial control Financing policy
Sustainable development / integrated planning	Biodiversity role in sustainable development	Sustainable development Commissions/ committees and their equivalent (e.g. cross-sectoral planning agencies) - if existing	Integrated policy across policy areas
Agriculture	Agricultural biodiversity (e.g. pollinators) Soil biodiversity Genetic resources Impacts on biodiversity	Agriculture (and food) ministry or department	Biodiversity based solutions to increase productivity Reducing externalities

TABLE 1 continued

POLICY-MAKER/ USER GROUP	BIODIVERSITY-RELATED INTERESTS	AGENCIES/INSTITUTIONS/ PERSONNEL	ROLE OF NATURAL CAPITAL ACCOUNTING IN IDENTIFYING:
Energy	Bioenergy Water regulation Reducing footprints Greenhouse gases		Biodiversity based solutions Reducing externalities
Tourism	Ecotourism	Tourism ministry/department	Nature based business National parks and nature areas
Transport	Impacts on biodiversity		Planning sustainable transport infrastructure and operation
Urban planning	Green/natural infrastructure and nature based solutions Urban biodiversity	Urban planning authorities (usually local)	Integrating biodiversity in urban planning solutions and reducing external impacts of cities
Education	Raise knowledge /awareness of the role of biodiversity in society	Education ministry/department	Educational curricula
OTHERS :			
Business	How biodiversity affects business models	Boards of directors, chief executive officers, chief financial officers, accounting and auditing personnel	Corporate social and environmental responsibility Efficient business models Reducing externalities and achieving resource use efficiencies
Research	Knowledge base on biodiversity and relevant policy tools	Academia, research institutes etc.	Improved knowledge base, developing effective tools
Media	News worthy biodiversity stories	Relevant media ministry/departments and media organizations	Communication strategies, public interest
Consumers (the "public")	Safe nutritious diets/ physical and mental health/ a safe and valuable natural environment/ sustainable development/ human well-being and happiness	Consumer support/representative agencies/organizations	Wise consumer choices to influence markets and production

ANNEX 2: AN INTRODUCTION TO THE SYSTEM OF ENVIRONMENTAL-ECONOMIC ACCOUNTING

Introduction to the SEEA methodology

The System of Environmental-Economic Accounting (SEEA) is the accepted international standard for natural capital accounting and provides a framework for organizing and presenting statistics on the environment and its relationship with the economy.

The SEEA framework follows a similar accounting structure as the System of National Accounts (SNA), which is the statistical standard to measure macro-economic transactions and flows. The SEEA framework uses concepts, definitions and classifications consistent with the SNA in order to facilitate the integration of environmental and economic statistics.

Two different perspectives are embodied in the SEEA. The first perspective is expressed through the SEEA-Central Framework (SEEA-CF), which looks at individual environmental assets such as energy, water, forests and timber, to explore how they are extracted from the environment, used in the economy, and returned to the environment in the form of waste, water and air emissions. The SEEA Central Framework allows for the integration of environmental information (often measured in physical terms) with economic information (often measured in monetary terms) in a single framework. The power of the SEEA Central Framework comes from its capacity to present information in both physical and monetary terms coherently. The SEEA-CF was adopted by the UN Statistical Commission, the apex body of the global statistical system, as the first international standard for environmental-economic accounting in 2012.

The second perspective complements the SEEA-CF by taking the perspective of ecosystems. The SEEA-Experimental Ecosystem Accounting (SEEA-EEA) looks at how individual environmental assets interact as part of natural processes within a given spatial area. The SEEA-EEA constitutes an integrated statistical framework for organizing biophysical data, measuring ecosystem services, tracking changes in ecosystem assets and linking this information to economic and other human activity. The SEEA-EEA was first drafted in 2012 and is now undergoing a revision, with the intention of reaching an agreement on as many aspects of ecosystem accounting as possible by the end of 2020.

SEEA-Central Framework

At the heart of the SEEA-CF is a systems approach to the organization of environmental and economic information which covers, as completely as possible, the stocks and flows that are relevant to the analysis of environmental and economic issues.

The SEEA-CF brings together, in a single measurement system, information natural resources, pollution and waste, production, consumption and accumulation. The SEEA-CF is composed of several subsystems which focus on specific areas of policy interest. For example, SEEA-Water is the conceptual framework and set of accounts which present hydrological information alongside economic information. SEEA-Water supports the analyses of the role of water within the economy and of the relationship between the environment and water-related activities, thereby supporting integrated water management. Other subsystems include agriculture, forestry and fisheries; air emissions; energy; environmental activity; land; material flow; and waste.

In practice, environmental-economic accounting includes the compilation of physical and monetary supply and use tables, functional accounts (such as environmental protection expenditure, taxes and subsidies accounts) and physical and monetary asset accounts. To assess how the economy supplies and uses natural inputs, SEEA accounts disaggregate flows by different units of production (industries as categorized by the International Standard Industrial Classification[17] and households). Data for SEEA accounts is usually collected from business and household surveys related to resource extraction and use.

SUPPLY AND USE TABLES

Supply and use tables in the SEEA-CF record the flows of natural inputs (e.g. flows of minerals, timber, fish and water), products and residuals (e.g. solid waste, air emissions and return flows of water) in both physical and monetary terms. In recording these flows, the SEEA-CF provides information on the amount and value of materials, water and energy that enter and leave the economy and flows of materials, water and energy within the economy itself. By providing information disaggregated by industries and households, supply and use tables provide valuable information on production and consumption patterns and changes in these patterns over time, as well as changes in the productivity and intensity of the use of natural inputs and the release of residuals.

Figure 1. Physical flows of natural inputs, products and residuals

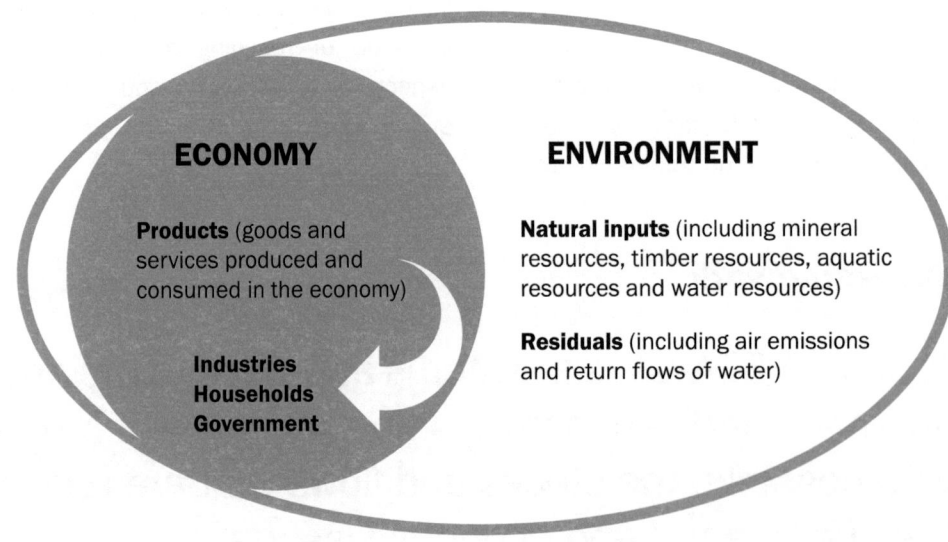

Source: SEEA-Central Framework (United Nations et al., 2014a)

[17] See https://unstats.un.org/unsd/publication/seriesM/seriesm_4rev4e.pdf.

ASSET ACCOUNTS

Stocks and changes in stocks of environmental assets (e.g. water, timber, fish, minerals and energy resources etc.) are measured in the SEEA-CF through asset accounts. In physical terms, the Central Framework focuses on recording the physical stocks and changes of stocks of individual environmental assets, such as tonnes of coal, cubic metres of timber and hectares of land. However, the SEEA-CF also includes the measurement of stocks in monetary terms. The measurement of stocks in monetary terms focuses on the value of individual environmental assets and changes in those values over time. The valuation of these assets focuses on the net present value of the benefits that accrue to economic owners of environmental assets, and the use of monetary terms enables the analysis of trade-offs between the conservation and use of different natural inputs.

ENVIRONMENTAL ACTIVITY ACCOUNTS

Environmental activity accounts are a subsystem of the SEEA-CF which deserve special mention, as they do not focus on individual environmental assets, but transactions taken to preserve and protect the environment. More specifically, environmental activity accounts record transactions in monetary terms between economic units that may be considered for environmental purposes. Generally, these transactions concern activity undertaken to preserve and protect the environment or activity designed to influence the behaviour of producers and consumers with respect to the environment. Environmental activity accounts in the SEEA-CF include environmental protection and resource management expenditure accounts (which include, for example, direct expenditures for the protection of biodiversity), environmental goods and services sector accounts, and environmental taxes and subsidies accounts. Used in tandem with other SEEA accounts, environmental activity accounts supply valuable information on whether economic resources are being used effectively to reduce pressures on the environment and maintain the capacity of the environment to deliver economic benefits.

SEEA-Experimental Ecosystem Accounting

Fundamental to ecosystem accounting is the recognition that ecosystems are the source of goods and services that are essential to economic prosperity and human well-being, now and in the future. In the SEEA, an ecosystem is defined as "a dynamic complex of plant, animal and micro-organism communities and their non-living environment interacting as a functional unit" (United Nations et al., 2014).[18]

---

[18] The SEEA uses the definition of the Convention on Biological Diversity. See https://www.cbd.int/ecosystem/description.shtml.

Ecosystem assets are areas covered by a specific ecosystem type, such as forests, wetlands, agricultural areas, rivers, coral reefs etc. The contributions of ecosystems range from natural products such as timber and game to services like purification of air and water, pollination of crops, nutrient cycling, carbon storage and more. The importance of these services underlines the need for a thorough understanding of the ways in which ecosystems support economic and social well-being.

The framework, which is well aligned to national accounting principles, allows for the measurement of ecosystem assets in terms of both their condition (overall health) and the services they provide, and can be applied consistently across terrestrial, freshwater and marine areas. A defining characteristic of ecosystem accounting is that it is spatially explicit, i.e., it builds accounts based on underlying maps with information. As such, ecosystem accounting produces an integrated spatial information system.

Ecosystem accounting is based upon the conceptual model shown in Figure 2. The model starts with identifying ecosystem assets - an ecosystem that is mapped by mutually exclusive spatial boundaries such that each asset is classified to a single ecosystem type. Assets can be described through their condition and extent. Through intra-and-inter ecosystem flows, ecosystem assets generate ecosystem services – the contributions of ecosystems to benefits used in economic and other human activity, for example water regulation.

Figure 2. *SEEA-EEA Conceptual Model*

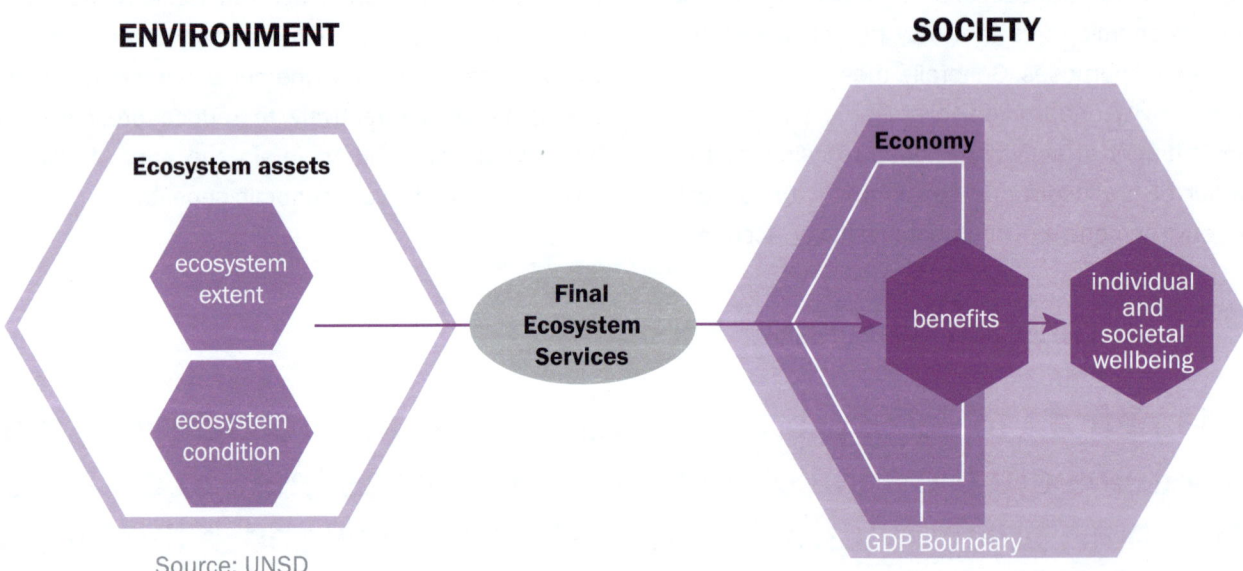

Source: UNSD

ECOSYSTEM EXTENT ACCOUNTS

Ecosystem extent accounts serve as a common starting point for ecosystem accounting. They organize information on the extent of different ecosystem types within a country in terms of area. In particular, ecosystem extent accounts describe the environment in terms of sets of mutually exclusive (i.e. non-overlapping) ecosystem assets. These assets (e.g. an individual forest, or a specific wetland) can be classified in terms of different ecosystem types such as forests, wetlands, cropland etc. All assets together populate an ecosystem accounting area, which could range from a watershed to a municipality to a country etc. The extent account describes the various types of ecosystems that are distinguished within an area and how they change over time.

ECOSYSTEM CONDITION ACCOUNTS

Condition accounts measure the overall quality of an ecosystem asset and capture, in a set of key indicators, the state or functioning of the ecosystem in relation to both its naturalness and its potential to supply ecosystem services. Essential is that the condition account compares at least two different years to track changes over time. As with all ecosystem accounts, condition accounts are built up from underlying maps of the various variables. For every ecosystem type (e.g. forests, inland water bodies etc.), a reference level is provided against which values for indicators can be compared. There is a wide range of indicators that can be assessed in the condition account, and indicators can be ecosystem type specific. Condition accounts provide valuable information on the health and state of ecosystems and their capacity of ecosystems to deliver critical ecosystem services in the future.

ECOSYSTEM SERVICES ACCOUNTS

This set of ecosystem accounts measures the supply of ecosystem services as well as their corresponding use and beneficiaries, classified by economic sectors used in the national accounts, in both physical and monetary terms. In SEEA EEA, ecosystem services are defined as "the contributions of ecosystems to benefits used in economic and other human activity" (United Nations et al, 2014b). SEEA EEA uses the following three broadly agreed categories of ecosystem services:

- Provisioning services (e.g. supply of food, fibre, fuel and water);

- Regulating services (related to activities of filtration, purification, regulation and maintenance of air, water, soil, habitat and climate); and

- Cultural services (related to activities of individuals in, or associated with, nature, such as recreation).

Ecosystem services are defined in SEEA EEA as the contribution to benefits, rather than as the benefits themselves, in order to avoid double counting. For example, an agricultural crop such as corn or maize is already recorded in the national accounts. Moreover, corn is the result of combining human capital (in the form of labour), produced capital (machinery) and natural capital (the cropland). The objective of the services accounts is to isolate the contributions of nature to the production of the crop visible. In addition, by expanding the national accounts production boundary, the accounts also recognize a range of ecosystem services that lead to benefits that are not currently recognized in the SNA such as carbon sequestration or air filtration.

MONETARY ASSET ACCOUNT

The monetary asset account records the monetary value of opening and closing stocks of all ecosystem assets within a given ecosystem accounting area, as well as additions and reduction to those stocks. The ecosystem services supply accounts are a key input into the monetary asset account and provide an estimate of the total annual flow that is generated during a specific year. The value of the ecosystem assets can be estimated by capitalizing these annual flows of services over the projected period i.e. the expected lifetime of the ecosystem, using a so-called net present value method. In order to estimate these projected service flows, it is important to take into account the capacity of the ecosystems to sustain these service flows which will depend on their condition and the extent to which these ecosystems are sustainably managed, and if not, make corrections to future service flows. Thus, the valuation of ecosystem assets allows an assessment of a more comprehensive measure of wealth of a country (in addition to produced capital, financial capital etc.).

THEMATIC ACCOUNTS

The SEEA-EEA also includes several thematic accounts. These are standalone accounts, or sets of accounts, that organize data according to an accounting framing about themes of specific policy relevance. For example, species accounts in the SEEA-EEA have the structure of an asset account and describe the opening and closing stock of a particular species over a period of time. The account tries to explain the observed changes in a number of categories (e.g. additions / reductions). The account can be compiled for instance for endangered species or for specific iconic species.

Carbon accounts are another common thematic account. The carbon account was developed to allow for a consistent and quantitative comparison of carbon stocks and flows in the reservoirs 'biocarbon' (organic carbon in soils and biomass), 'geocarbon' (carbon in the lithosphere), atmospheric carbon and carbon in the economy. Other potential thematic accounts include accounting for protected areas, wetlands and forests.

Aggregates and indicators

The SEEA-CF and SEEA-EEA are multipurpose and relevant in a number of ways for policy development and evaluation, as well as decision-making. First, the summary information (provided in the form of aggregates and indicators) can be applied to issues and areas of the environment that are the focus of decision makers. For instance, the SEEA-CF and SEEA-EEA provide the data to inform 40 SDG indicators, including goals 2, 6, 7, 8, 9, 11, 12, 14 and 15.

Second, the detailed information, which covers some of the key drivers of change in the environment, can be used to provide a richer understanding of the policy issues. For example, the SEEA-CF accounts can be effectively communicated to users and decision makers through combined presentations combining physical and monetary data. A combined presentation thus represents an analytical framework showing which parts of the economy are most relevant to specific aspects of the environment, and how changes in the economic structure influence the environment (see Figure 3).

Figure 3. *Possible structure of and typical content for combined presentations*

	Industries (by ISIC divisions)	Households	Government	Accumulation	Flows with the rest of the world	Total
Monetary supply and use: flows						
(currency units)						
Supply of products						
Intermediate consumption and final use of products						
Gross value added						
Depletion-adjusted value added						
Environmental taxes, subsidies and similar transfers						
Physical supply and use: flows						
(physical units)						
Supply of:						
Natural inputs						
Products						
Residuals						
Use of:						
Natural inputs						
Products						
Residuals						
Asset stocks and flows						
Closing stocks of environmental assets						
(currency units and physical units)						
Depletion (currency units and physical units)						
Closing stocks of fixed assets (currency units)						
Gross fixed capital formation (currency units)						
Related socio-demographic data						
Employment						
Population						

Note: Dark grey cells are null by definition

Source: SEEA-Central Framework (United Nations, 2014a).

Further, as the accounts provide consistent environmental and economic indicators, the possible trade-offs in environmental terms between alternative environmental and economic strategies can be analysed. The SEEA enables the calculation of indicators on several topics, including: resource use and intensity; production, employment and expenditure related to environmental activities; environmental taxes and environmental subsidies; and environmental assets, wealth, income and depletion of resources.

The SEEA also enables the derivation of depletion-adjusted balancing items and aggregates within the sequence of economic accounts of the SNA. Using the SEEA, balancing items, within the sequence of economic accounts, can be adjusted for depletion so that estimates of the monetary cost of using up natural resources can be deducted from conventional economic aggregates, such as GDP and saving to yield depletion-adjusted aggregates.

Applications of the SEEA

There are several other applications of the SEEA.[19] One common application of the SEEA is environmentally extended input-output tables (EE-IOT). EE-IOT are datasets that combine information from economic input-output tables from the SNA in monetary units and information on environmental flows, such as flows of natural inputs and residuals, that are measured in physical units.

EE-IOT data sets, which reflect industry and product detail in physical and monetary terms and encompass economic and environmental information, can be powerful tools in analysis and research. Input-output analysis is regularly used to attribute environmental flows to final demand categories. It can identify the link between final demand and resource use, emissions and other environmentally related flows and thereby highlighting "hot spots" or "pressure points" that are highly policy relevant.

The SEEA is also often used for decomposition analysis, a tool which enables separate estimates of the particular drivers influencing changes in environmental impacts or pressures. Since changes in the pressures from the environment occur within dynamic systems of interactions, it is often difficult to identify the extent to which specific consumption and production activities have contributed to changes in environmental impacts or pressures. Decomposition analysis can be used to account in detail for the factors underlying these changes. Typically, the variables used in the calculations include changes in the size of the economy, changes in the structure of the supply chain and demand, changes in the energy intensity of production, and improvements in the production process. Decomposition analysis can be used to understand, for example, the economic or technological changes that have caused emissions of CO_2 to increase. Thus, decomposition analysis can be a powerful tool for analysis and policy design.

Finally, another common application of the SEEA is computable general equilibrium (CGE) models. CGE models are a class of economic models that combine use of input-output data with the application of microeconomic theory and are especially well suited to analysing the future effects of policies. They consist of a system of non-linear demand, supply and market equilibrium equations, into which various assumptions may be introduced (depending on the model). In the context of the SEEA, CGE models may be developed using information contained in EE-IOT, thus bringing together monetary and physical data. The use of CGE models can facilitate an understanding of what dynamic impacts may be expected in the case of policy interventions, or other developments. For example, CGE models can assist in understanding the dynamics arising from the introduction of a tax on CO_2 emissions, which will entail a shift away from relatively carbon-intensive inputs.

---

[19] See The System of Evnironmental-Economic Accounting 2012 Applications and Extensions, https://seea.un.org/sites/seea.un.org/files/ae_final_en.pdf.